NEW ZEALAND

BY SUE BRADFORD EDWARDS

An Imprint of Abdo Publishing
abdobooks.com

ABDOBOOKS.COM
Published by Abdo Publishing, a division of ABDO, PO Box 398166, Minneapolis, Minnesota 55439.

Printed in China.
052025
092025

Cover Photo: Natalia Ramirez Roman/500Px Plus/Getty Images (cliffs); Shutterstock Images (pattern)
Interior Photos: iStockphoto, 4–5, 59, 77, 93; Shutterstock Images, 7, 11, 14–15, 16 (right), 20, 26–27, 28–29, 36, 44, 52–53, 62–63, 64–65, 69, 73, 84–85, 96–97, 98, 101; Marcel Strelow/Shutterstock Images, 12; Red Line Editorial, 16 (left); Uwe Aranas/Shutterstock Images, 19; Keystone Pictures USA/Keystone Press/Alamy, 24; Ross Gordon Henry/Shutterstock Images, 30; Science History Images/Alamy, 32; Kamila Koziol/Shutterstock Images, 35; Boris Pamikov/Shutterstock Images, 38–39; Sentilo Media/Alamy, 40–41; Pictures from History/Universal Images Group/Getty Images, 42; Lakeview Images/Alamy, 47; DEA/Biblioteca Ambrosiana/De Agostini/Getty Images, 48; Torsten Blackwood/AFP/Getty Images, 50; Aroon Thaewchatturat/Alamy, 56; Jiri Hera/Shutterstock Images, 60; Hagen Hopkins/Getty Images News/Getty Images, 67, 72; Hagen Hopkins/Getty Images Entertainment/Getty Images, 70; Tomas Pavelka/Shutterstock Images, 74–75; Daniela Schroeder/Shutterstock Images, 79; Dmitry Pichugin/Shutterstock Images, 80; Kai Schwoerer/Getty Images Sport/Getty Images, 86; John Norman/Alamy, 90; Mike Dickison/Wikimedia Commons, 92; Todd Strand/Alamy, 95

Editor: Marley Richmond
Series Designer: Maggie Villaume

Library of Congress Control Number: 2024948568

PUBLISHER'S CATALOGING-IN-PUBLICATION DATA
Names: Edwards, Sue Bradford, author.
Title: New Zealand / by Sue Bradford Edwards
Description: Minneapolis, Minnesota: Abdo Publishing, 2026 | Series: Essential library of countries | Includes online resources and index.
Identifiers: ISBN 9781098297008 (lib. bdg.) | ISBN 9798384919520 (ebook)
Subjects: LCSH: Geography--Juvenile literature. | New Zealand--Juvenile literature. | Islands of the Pacific--Juvenile literature. | New Zealand--History--Juvenile literature.
Classification: DDC 993--dc23

CONTENTS

CHAPTER **ONE**

A TOUR OF NEW ZEALAND

Luke stretched his neck as he followed his parents out of the airport. They had left San Francisco, California, 13 hours earlier. Their final destination would be Rotorua, New Zealand, but they first had a layover in Auckland, New Zealand. The sun was above the skyline, and the clock above the terminal's exit doors showed it was almost 8:00 a.m. Luke and his parents wanted to experience some of the city before catching their next flight.

Luke's father messaged a taxi service, and soon they were on their way across the city. He directed the driver to take them to the Auckland Botanic Gardens, and

Auckland is a port city where many important goods are shipped into New Zealand. Waitematā Harbour borders the city to the north.

15 minutes later the family had arrived. There was no admission fee to enter the garden. The three of them walked to the garden's restaurant, Café Miko, for breakfast. They all agreed to try something they didn't usually eat at home.

Luke glanced at the menu and grinned. "I'll have Indonesian nasi goreng," he said. "That's fried rice with vegetables, prawn crackers, and a fried egg," he told his parents. Luke's father ordered shakshuka—eggs poached in a sauce of beans and tomatoes, served with toast. His mother selected homemade granola with yogurt. She wanted to see what fruit the dish included and discovered that she got to choose raisins, apricots, or cacao and coconut. The three of them sipped water and espresso as they enjoyed their breakfasts, and soon they were ready to explore.

PIKELETS AND PANCAKES

Some foods have different names around the world. Pancakes are called pikelets in New Zealand, and they tend to be smaller than US pancakes. They are served with butter or whipped cream and jam. Restaurants also serve foods called pancakes, but they are more like heavy crepes. New Zealand pancakes come with savory toppings such as vegetables in cheese sauce or chicken and mushrooms.

AUCKLAND

As Luke exited the café with his parents, he was surprised to see people jogging and walking their dogs inside the botanic garden. There were even people sitting on the grass, drinking from their water bottles and having conversations. "This seems more like a park than the botanical garden back home," Luke said. A passing staff member explained that bicycles and skateboards weren't allowed, but otherwise the garden was very similar to a park.

Luke strolled between tidy garden beds that reminded him of gardens back home. His parents spotted rock gardens and a colorful rose garden before they reached a section of massive trees that looked like nothing they had ever seen before. The sign read "Gondwana Arboretum." The area reminded Luke of a forest rather than a garden, since it had more trees than flowers.

Luke's mom explained that Gondwana was an ancient supercontinent made up of all the landmasses in today's Southern Hemisphere. She told Luke about a video she watched that had been produced by the Auckland Botanic Gardens. It explained that the trees in the arboretum are similar to trees from 200 million years ago.

She pointed out a monkey puzzle tree. It was covered in spiky leaves that kept animals from

The Chatham Island nīkau is a palm tree unique to New Zealand. It grows in the Auckland Botanic Gardens' Native Plant Ideas garden.

eating it. The Gondwana Arboretum contains trees from Africa and Australia, but Luke's family wanted to see a native New Zealand tree, the kauri.

Luke's family found the kauri trees and gazed up at the straight trunks. "How long do you think they can live?" Luke asked. He squinted up at the leathery, oval leaves that ranged in color from copper to green. Their smooth texture contrasted against the tree's rough, gray bark.

"The video said they can reach 2,500 years old, but now some of the trees are dying because of kauri dieback disease.[1] Fortunately, the garden is researching ways to treat trees that become infected," his mom said.

Luke stared up into the trees and then hurried to catch up with his parents. Eventually he and his parents reached the Puhinui Stream Forest Trail. The trail took Luke's family through a remnant forest, part of the original forest that covered New Zealand. Luke felt lucky he could see these historic trees the garden had preserved as part of the arboretum.

The first interesting tree Luke spotted had drooping branches similar to those of a weeping willow. But unlike those of a willow, the branches of the rimu tree were covered with evergreen needles. Luke also spotted many interesting plants called tree ferns. They had tree trunks topped with leafy fronds. Eventually the family completed their hike by exiting through Totara Park.

THE AUCKLAND ART GALLERY

Luke's family stopped for a quick lunch before heading to their next destination. This time they selected a vegan café, where Luke opted for coconut curry with tofu. His mother ordered shepherd's pie, which was a combination of vegetables baked under mashed potatoes, and his father picked out a spicy dal, an Indian dish made with lentils. When their dishes came, they took turns sampling each other's choices. When they were finished, they walked over to the Auckland Art Gallery.

Luke wandered the free gallery looking at many types of art. His mother liked the exhibit showing paintings and photographs of New Zealand's coastline, but Luke's favorites were the futuristic sculptures by Simon Denny. These were inspired by sketches of fuel systems for rockets created by the New Zealand–founded aerospace company Rocket Lab. Luke especially liked one that resembled a gear-shaped spaceship.

In 2023, 2.96 million visitors came to New Zealand.[2]

ROTORUA

Luke would have preferred to travel by train to the town of Rotorua, but his parents decided it would be easier to fly. They boarded a flight that lasted less than an hour. After checking in to their hotel, they walked to Kuirau Park. It featured a pretty lake, but Luke wasn't sure why his parents were so excited. As he followed them farther into the park, he saw a small, natural pool of steaming water.

His father said that Kuirau is one of several parks in Rotorua with geothermal activity. He explained that heat from Earth's crust warms up water or mud, which was why the water they saw was steaming. Luke spotted the nearby signs that read, "Danger, keep to the track, gases, hot area, unstable ground." His father reminded them all that a few years earlier a new vent had opened and shot football-sized pieces of rock into the air. Luke wondered aloud whether they might get to see something similar.

Some areas of Kuirau Park featured barren rocks with steam emerging from between stones. Others had natural ponds with mossy banks, where the waterfalls and water steamed. There were even bubbling pools of heated mud.

As Luke and his parents exited the park, they spotted people sitting around a rectangular pool. People had taken off their shoes and socks and were soaking their feet in the heated water. Luke dropped to the ground and pulled off his boots, sighing as he submerged his feet.

Afterward the family returned to the hotel for a light supper. They made selections from the dim sum menu, which featured small dishes for the family to share. The menu had a traditional array of Chinese foods such as dumplings, buns, prawns, and barbecue pork. Each of them ordered several dishes to try. Luke ordered fried dim sim, a type of Chinese-inspired dumpling filled with pork and prawns unique to New Zealand and Australia.

Night was falling when Luke and his family headed down to the city's visitor's center, where a

GLOWWORMS

New Zealand's glowworms aren't actually worms but the larval form of a gnat, *Arachnocampa luminosa*, that looks similar to a mosquito. The larvae live on cave roofs, where they are fastened by mucus they secrete. Their blue-green glow is created by an enzyme called luciferase. Their glow attracts potential prey that get stuck to strings of sticky silk hanging below the larvae. The larvae reel in and then digest the captured insects. The gnats live in this larval phase for about one year.

Paths lead visitors around and across geothermal ponds throughout Kuirau Park. People can see the steam rise from the heated water.

kayaking guide met them along with a larger group of tourists. Everyone put on a life jacket and got into a kayak. The group followed the guide along the shore and then paddled into a cave. People gasped as they looked up. Glowworms were scattered across the ceiling. The glowworms looked so similar to stars that it took Luke a minute to notice when he had moved back out onto the lake. The sky overhead was awash in starlight like nothing Luke had seen in his entire life.

Glowworms living in caves create silk strands that are up to about 20 inches (50 cm) long.

Luke attempted to pick out the Big Dipper, Orion, or another of the constellations he could recognize, but he couldn't spot any of them. Then he listened to what the guide was saying as she reminded visitors from the Northern Hemisphere that Southern Hemisphere constellations were completely different. She pointed to the stars that marked the ends of the arms of the Southern Cross, a constellation that is part of New Zealand's flag. Luke gazed up in awe, excited to discover more of the country's wonders.

A NATION OF ISLANDS

New Zealand lies in the Southern Hemisphere, or the southern half of Earth. There, the seasons are reversed compared to those in the Northern Hemisphere. In the Southern Hemisphere, summer starts in December, and winter starts in June.

New Zealand is in the southern Pacific Ocean in an area known as Oceania. Its nearest neighbor, Australia, is 1,000 miles (1,600 km) away. New Zealand is a nation of islands, comprised of two large islands and additional small islands. Some of these smaller islands are more than 100 miles (161 km) from the main islands.[3] The country's remote location allowed the plants and animals that live there to develop in isolation. Many species in New Zealand are not found anywhere else on Earth.

The area was first populated by the ancestors of the Māori, the Indigenous people of New Zealand. Colonizers and immigrants came later from the United Kingdom and other parts of the world. Over time, people in New Zealand developed a culture that emphasizes life in the outdoors and welcomes visitors from all around the world.

OCEANIA

As the name suggests, most of Oceania is ocean. Of the area's 38.6 million square miles (100 million sq km), only 3.3 million square miles (8.5 million sq km) is land.[4] Some islands are called low or coral islands. They barely rise above sea level. Others are called high or volcanic islands. These have built up over time when volcanic lava flows and cools. The ecosystems found on volcanic islands are diverse and include deserts, mangrove swamps, forests, and coral reefs.

CHAPTER **TWO**

GEOGRAPHY

New Zealand measures 1,000 miles (1,600 km) from north to south and 280 miles (450 km) across at its widest point.[1] This nation is part of Oceania, also known as the Pacific Islands, which consists of three sections: Micronesia, Melanesia, and Polynesia. New Zealand is part of Polynesia, a triangular region that stretches from New Zealand in the southwest to the US state of Hawaii in the north and Easter Island in the southeast.

New Zealand's area is 103,799 square miles (268,838 sq km), which includes land and water.[2] It is approximately the same total area as the US state of Colorado. New Zealand includes approximately 600 islands, although official counts vary slightly, and many of New Zealand's islands are uninhabited.[3]

Turquoise-blue glacial lakes sit within the Southern Alps on New Zealand's South Island.

MAP OF NEW ZEALAND

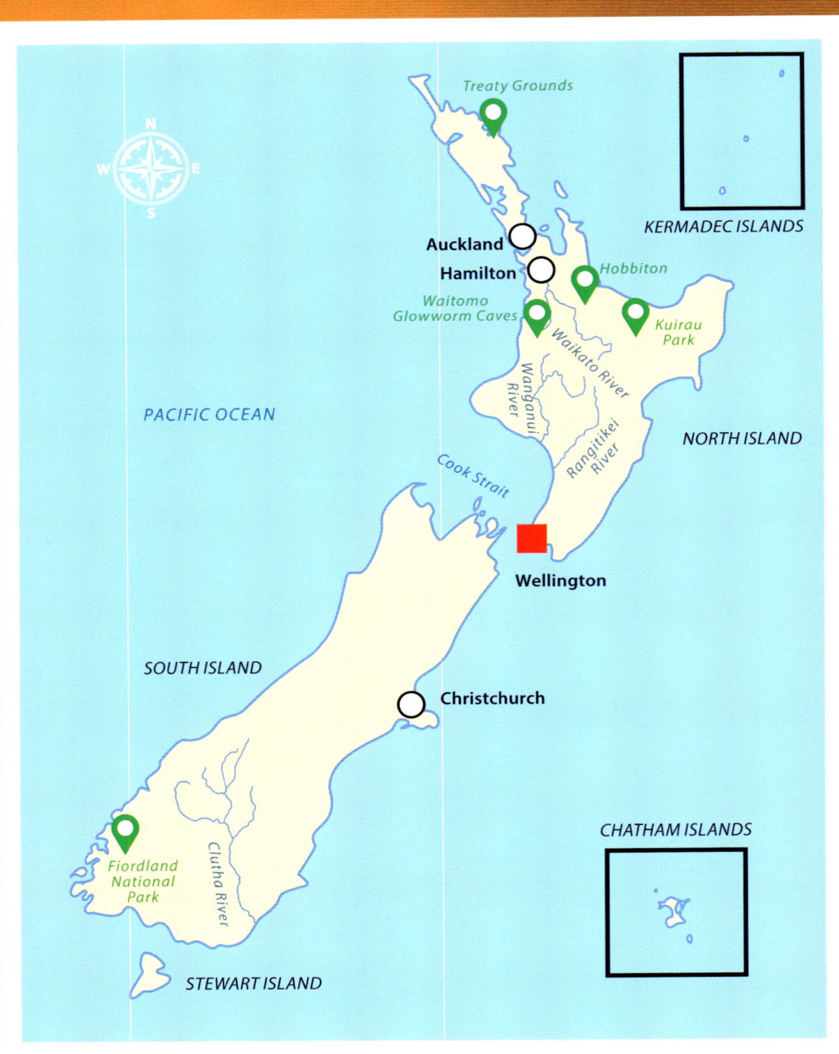

KEY:

- Capital
- City
- Point of Interest

The nation has two main islands. North Island is approximately 44,872 square miles (116,218 sq km).[4] South Island is a bit larger at approximately 58,776 square miles (152,229 sq km).[5] These two islands are separated by the Cook Strait.

CLIMATE

Summer in New Zealand is December through February, and winter is June through August. In general, the summer temperature ranges from 50 to 75 degrees Fahrenheit (10–24°C), and in winter it ranges from 35 to 50 degrees Fahrenheit (2–10°C).[6] North Island has slightly warmer temperatures than South Island. Throughout South Island's mountains, the temperatures can be especially cold and windy.

New Zealand's climate varies because of ocean currents and mountains. Although most of the country gets between 23 and 63 inches (58–160 cm) of rain per year, some areas on the west coast can receive as much rain as 300 inches (762 cm) each year.[7] The driest parts of the country are east of the mountains. In northern and central New Zealand, most of the rain falls in winter, but in southern New Zealand there is less rain in the winter. The sunniest parts of the country include Bay of Plenty, Marlborough, and Hawke's Bay.

Most of New Zealand's snowfall occurs from June through October. The Southern Alps and Central Plateau receive the majority of the snow because both areas are mountainous, where high elevations and cold temperatures make snow common. The highest peaks in the Southern Alps are snowcapped year-round.

NORTH ISLAND

With coastlines surrounding every island, New Zealand has a wide variety of beaches. Most of those on the east coast of North Island are sandy and frequented by swimmers and surfers. The beaches on the island's west coast are black. The color comes from the iron that makes up part of the sand.

North Island rises into a series of mountain ranges that run parallel to the island's east coast and include the Tararua Range, the Ruahine Range, the Kaweka Range, the Huiarau Range, and the Raukūmara Range. To the northwest of the mountains, at the island's center, stands a volcanic plateau that is alive with volcanic and geothermal activity. Tall tussock grasslands, recognizable by their characteristic tufts of grass, cover this plateau.

Tussock grasses are species of grasses that grow in tall, feathery clumps. Below the mountain tree line, reddish copper tussock dominates the landscape, with clusters of tall blades that reach up to 39 inches (1 m) long.[8] Above the tree line, snow tussock is more common. Snow tussock is the name for several high-altitude species including curled snow tussock and snow patch-grass. Curled snow tussock grows in clusters with blades of grass that are much shorter than copper tussock. The tussock grasslands provide homes to communities of insects.

BLACK SAND

Most New Zealand sand that is tan colored is composed of ground-up shells and rock. Dark or black sand is composed of ground-up titanomagnetite, a mineral that combines both titanium and iron. Because of the iron, this sand is dark in color, and it is also magnetic. Magnet artists place magnets in patterns to manipulate the sand and create temporary sculptures on beaches.

Tussock grasslands cover one-fifth of New Zealand's landscape.

The water of the Clutha River comes from glaciers and snowmelt in the Southern Alps. Its water source and route give the Clutha River a bright blue color.

In addition to the tussock grasslands, North Island is home to various other biomes. Mangrove forests grow along the northern coast of North Island. Mangrove trees have adapted to being flooded by salt water twice daily at high tide and also being rooted in heavy mud that provides very little oxygen to the trees' roots.

North Island is also home to evergreen forests, where trees never drop their leaves. Beneath the trees, various ferns and mosses form the undergrowth. Mist shrouds the trees in Te Urewera. This is the island's largest rainforest, spreading across 821 square miles (2,127 sq km).[9]

The tallest mountain on North Island is Mount Ruapehu, an active volcano that is 9,175 feet (2,797 m) tall.[11]

Rivers and lakes are an important part of New Zealand's geography. The country's largest lake is on North Island. Taupō is 525 feet (160 m) deep. It fills the crater of an ancient volcano and is drained by the Waikato River, which is New Zealand's longest river at 264 miles (425 km). The next longest rivers are the Whanganui River at 180 miles long (290 km) and the Rangitikei River at 150 miles (241 km) long.[10]

SOUTH ISLAND

The northern end of South Island has some sandy beaches, while the rest of the island's coastline is rockier. South Island's two longest rivers are the Clutha River and the Taieri River. South Island also contains a variety of biomes. Like North Island, it is home to tussock grasslands that cover much of the eastern side of the island. Much of this area is now used as farmland and pastureland because of its rich soil.

South Island's forests are dominated by beech trees, which grow best in mountainous areas and continue to thrive because these areas have not been cleared for agriculture. About two-thirds of New Zealand's forests have at least some beech trees in them.[12] Beech forests provide habitats for mistletoe and various fungi.

South Island also has an alpine vegetation zone within the Southern Alps. These mountains, also known as Kā Tiritiri o te Moana, were formed by the movement of tectonic plates. Tectonic plates are large sections of Earth's crust that move slightly each year. One of these plates is the Australian Plate. As this plate moves against the Pacific Plate, the Australian Plate is pushed upward. Over a long period of time, this action formed the Southern Alps.

In the 1990s, the Southern Alps had more than 3,000 glaciers.[13] But this number has decreased due to climate change. Glaciers develop when the amount of winter snowfall exceeds the amount of snow that melts throughout the year. The weight of this slowly accumulating snow creates pressure that forms glacier ice.

Gravity drags the glacier slowly downhill, similar to a river. As glaciers move, they scour the landscape, scraping away dirt and soil and often leaving depressions. When a glacier melts, some of the depressions fill with melted glacier water and form glacial lakes. Two large glacial lakes within the Southern Alps are Pūkaki and Tekapo. Pūkaki is filled by the Tasman River, which flows from the Tasman Glacier, while the water in Tekapo comes from the Godley River, which flows from the Godley Glacier. New Zealand's glaciers are all melting at an increasing rate due to climate change.

The tallest mountain in New Zealand is Mount Cook at approximately 12,218 feet (3,724 m).[14]

VOLCANOES

New Zealand is within the Ring of Fire, an area where shifting tectonic plates meet and produce significant volcanic activity. The country is home to eight active volcanoes.[15] These volcanoes are fed by the same plate tectonics that created the Southern Alps.

As the Australian Plate moves against the Pacific Plate, the Pacific Plate is pushed down below Earth's crust and into the mantle. Under intense pressure and heat, the Pacific Plate melts into a molten material called magma. This magma can erupt to the surface from any of New Zealand's active volcanoes.

The time between eruptions for a specific volcano can be anywhere from several years to thousands of years. Scientists carefully monitor the volcanoes for signs of eruptions. Some of New Zealand's volcanoes are near cities or towns.

The Auckland Volcanic Field is a cluster volcano with 53 volcanic centers scattered around Auckland.[16] These centers are locations where lava may erupt. Each time there has been an eruption, it

FIORDLAND NATIONAL PARK

Fiordland National Park is located in the southwestern corner of South Island. Fiord is another spelling of the word *fjord*, and the park encompasses the island's fjords, which are U-shaped indentations carved by glaciers and flooded by the sea. The deepest fjord, Doubtful Sound, provides a home for penguins, fur seals, and bottlenose dolphins. In 1990, the park was recognized by the United Nations Educational, Scientific and Cultural Organization (UNESCO) as a World Heritage site, a place of great value to humanity. It was named Te Wahipounamu, or "the place of green stone" in the Māori language, because of the deposits of stone found there and valued by the Māori.

EDMUND HILLARY

Edmund Hillary was born on July 20, 1919, in Auckland, New Zealand. In high school, Hillary climbed New Zealand's Southern Alps. After he served in World War II (1939–1945), he decided to climb Mount Everest in the Himalayas, a major mountain range in central Asia. Hillary and his guide, Tenzing Norgay, would be the first people to summit the world's tallest mountain.

In 1951, Hillary was a member of a New Zealand party climbing the Himalayas. He joined a mountaineering team that would attempt to reach Everest's summit in 1953. In mid-May, the group established a high camp where the climbers could acclimate to the altitude and then attempt the summit.

Two other climbers had been chosen for the first attempt to summit Everest, but they turned around before reaching the top because they were low on oxygen, which climbers often use at high elevations when the air grows thin. Three days later, Hillary was paired with Sherpa guide Tenzing Norgay, the group's most experienced climber. Hillary navigated a tall, tunnellike gap in the rock, and the pair reached the mountain's summit at 11:30 a.m. on May 29, 1953.

Edmund Hillary, *left*, and Sherpa Tenzing Norgay, *right*, celebrated summiting Mount Everest together.

has occurred at a new location. Although the volcanic field is active, scientists consider it to be at low risk of eruption, and some of the centers are now public parks.

Other volcanoes have shaped the landscape in surprising ways. Taupō is a caldera volcano. Calderas form when a volcano erupts and leaves the stone chamber that held magma empty. If this chamber collapses, it creates a caldera, or bowl, which may fill with water and create a lake. Taupō's most recent eruption was 1,800 years ago.[17]

Raoul Island is a volcanic island formed by an underwater volcano that extends above sea level, located 621 miles (1,000 km) northeast of New Zealand's main islands. It last erupted on March 17, 2006, at 8:20 in the morning, ejecting rock and mud for 30 minutes.[18] There were no warning signs that an eruption was imminent, but scientists now believe that an earthquake triggered the eruption. Raoul Island is a composite volcano, meaning the cone built up over several eruptions. This type of volcano may be active for hundreds of thousands of years.

Raoul is one of the Kermadec Islands, which are located 500 to 620 miles (800–1,000 km) northeast

RING OF FIRE

The Ring of Fire is a horseshoe-shaped expanse of seismic, or earthquake-related, activity in the Pacific Ocean. It is also known as the Circum-Pacific Belt. It extends for 24,900 miles (40,000 km). The ring crosses New Zealand, Indonesia, the Philippines, Japan, and the west coasts of North America and South America. Along the Ring of Fire lie more than 450 volcanoes, which make up 75 percent of the world's volcanoes. Ninety percent of the world's earthquakes occur there.[19] Seismologists are scientists who study earthquakes, and they do not yet know how to predict these quakes along the Ring of Fire.

Whakaari, or White Island, is New Zealand's most active volcano. It erupted in 2019. Whakaari sits 30 miles (48 km) from North Island, so eruptions are unlikely to affect the mainland.

of North Island. The group consists of four islands and several large rocks. Raoul is the only island that is habitable, although all the people who live there study the island, including Department of Conservation staff and scientists. One of these staff members was killed when the volcano erupted in 2006.[20] New Zealand authorities take the risk posed by the nation's volcanoes seriously. Monitoring equipment keeps track of early warning signs, and visitors are warned of potential risk.

CHAPTER **THREE**

PLANTS AND ANIMALS

New Zealand is home to an estimated 80,000 species of plants, animals, and fungi.[1] Because New Zealand became isolated from other landmasses while species evolved, many of the nation's flora and fauna are endemic species. Endemic species live only in a limited area, such as a single country.

All the frogs and reptiles found in New Zealand are endemic, as are 90 percent of its insects and 80 percent of its vascular plants, including flowering plants and ferns.[2] Very few predatory mammals evolved in New Zealand, which meant that smaller animals and birds thrived. The lack of predators also explains why many of New Zealand's birds are flightless.

Several species of skinks, a type of reptile, are endemic to New Zealand, including the Barrier skink found on South Island.

Tuataras may be olive green, brown, or orangey red. They shed their skin once per year and can slowly change color over time.

LAND ANIMALS

The tuatara is New Zealand's largest reptile, averaging 20 to 31 inches (50–80 cm) in length.[3] Although it looks like a lizard, it is a different type of reptile that belongs to the order Sphenodontia. At the time of the dinosaurs, this order of reptiles thrived, but today the lone survivor is the tuatara. It has what some scientists refer to as a third eye, located on top of its head. This isn't a fully developed eye but rather a grouping of cells that helps the creature detect light.

Tuataras thrive in cooler weather compared with other reptiles and once lived across New Zealand. Today they live on only a few islands. They are active at night. On average, tuataras live for 60 years, although they can live for as long as 100 years.[4]

The only terrestrial mammals native to New Zealand are two species of bats, the long-tailed bat and the lesser short-tailed bat. Long-tailed bats live on New Zealand's two main islands as well as several smaller islands. They feed on flying insects and are considered a critically endangered species, meaning that they are at risk of extinction. A group of long-tailed bats may live across as many as 100 trees, so the Department of Conservation encourages people to preserve forestland, including dead trees.[5]

Reptiles, mammals, and birds in New Zealand are hunted by predators that people brought to the islands, including the three types of rats that can be found in New Zealand. Kiore, the first rats to arrive, came with traveling Māori and live on various islands. Norway rats and black rats came with whalers and European colonists. Another predator is the stoat, a member of the family Mustelidae that resembles its cousin the weasel. Stoats were intentionally brought to New Zealand in the 1870s to hunt rabbits, also imported, that were eating the grass that farmers wanted for their sheep. Cats were also released into the wild to hunt rabbits. Stoats and cats now hunt New Zealand's native insects, birds, and reptiles.

BIRDS

Because New Zealand's native animals evolved with no large predators, many birds lost the ability to fly because it wasn't needed to escape. Among New Zealand's flightless birds was the moa. Scientists debate how many species of moa existed, but they do know the smallest was about the size of a turkey, while the giant moa was bigger than an ostrich, standing ten feet (3 m) tall.[6]

Moa were grazers, and the Māori hunted them for food, made clothing from the birds' skins and feathers, and crafted fishhooks and pendants from the moa's bones. By the end of the 1600s, the giant moa had been hunted to extinction, and all moa were extinct by the 1800s.

A nickname for a New Zealander is a Kiwi, which comes from a well-known flightless bird native to the country. There are five species of kiwi. The smallest is the little spotted kiwi, which is 14 to 18 inches (35–45 cm) tall, while the largest is the brown kiwi at 20 to 25 inches (50–65 cm). Kiwi live in forested areas or grasslands and dig burrows where a female will lay up to six eggs annually.[7] The eggshells have antibacterial and antifungal properties to help prevent infection to unhatched kiwi, which would otherwise be common in the damp environment where the birds live. Dogs are a danger to adult birds, and stoats hunt kiwi chicks.

There are other flightless birds that live only in New Zealand. The takahē is the world's largest rail, a family of ground-dwelling birds with short wings and large feet. Scientists thought the takahē was extinct for nearly 50 years until 1948, when a man named Geoffrey Orbell found a wild population

HUIA

The huia was a large species of wattlebird that had glossy black feathers with long, white-tipped tail feathers. When the Duke of York was photographed wearing a tail feather in 1901, huia feathers became fashionable. Hunters skinned the birds, and zoos and collectors paid for living specimens. Imported predators also took a toll on the huia population. Although the government passed laws in 1892 to halt hunting, the laws were not enforced. The last huia was sighted in 1907, and the species is now extinct.

in Fiordland's mountain grasslands while hiking. New Zealanders set up sanctuaries, and by 2023 there were 500 takahē.[8]

Another endangered bird is the kākāpō, the world's heaviest parrot. Males weigh almost five pounds (2.2 kg) and females weigh about 3 pounds (1.4 kg).[9] Although these birds can't fly, they do climb and eat treetop fruits and vines. They also eat tubers they excavate from the ground.

Not all New Zealand birds are flightless. The morepork is a speckled brown owl with bright yellow eyes. Females are 11 inches (29 cm) long and normally lay two eggs between September and November.[10] Morepork live in forests and at night hunt primarily large invertebrates, including moths, beetles, spiders, and wētā. Wētā are hamster-sized insects that look similar to their cousins, crickets.

Another noteworthy New Zealand bird is the kea. This intelligent parrot lives in the mountains and forests of South Island. These birds have locked people inside restrooms at campgrounds and learned to turn on water taps. They eat seeds, buds, berries, and flowers. They also hunt small animals, which puts them at risk when people try to kill predators using poisoned bait. The New Zealand government considers this olive-green parrot to be nationally endangered.

PLANTS

New Zealand's plants also developed unique adaptations to the country's landscape, including divarication, a pattern of growth with tangled stems

Only 11 species of New Zealand plants are deciduous, meaning they lose their leaves in winter.[11]

and small leaves. Scientists believe divarication may keep plants' leaves tucked out of reach of grazing animals. The growth pattern may also protect the plant from frost or snow. One bush that grows in this way is the red-berried twiggy coprosma.

Small, white, fragrant flowers are another common adaptation seen in New Zealand's plants. The most common pollinators in New Zealand are moths, native bees, crawling insects, and lizards. These pollinators are drawn to a flower not by its color but by its scent, which means big showy flowers would be a waste of a plant's energy. Lemonwood trees are known for their lemon-scented leaves and small, pale flowers that give off a honey-like scent.

Lemonwood trees are dioecious. Dioecious trees produce male flowers on male trees and female flowers on female trees, rather than growing both male and female flowers on a single tree. This characteristic occurs more often in New Zealand's trees than in those in many other parts of the world. The trait brings greater genetic variability, which can help trees adapt to a changing environment.

One final adaptation is variability of form in a single plant species. Sometimes the juvenile and adult plants of a single species look different, which is called heteroblasty. This trait may provide

TĀNEKAHA

The New Zealand tānekaha is also known as the celery pine because people thought it looked like celery. What appear to be leaves are an ancient adaptation known as phylloclades, which are actually flattened stems. These flattened stems are where photosynthesis takes place, using a substance called chlorophyll to transform sunlight into energy. Despite this adaptation, the tānekaha tree does grow some tiny leaves that look similar to eyelashes, but they quickly drop off the tree.

different advantages to a plant at different stages of its growth. For example, plant shape and leaf size may vary between juvenile and adult stages to take advantage of light levels that change as the plant grows from the shaded forest floor to the sunny canopy. Kōwhai and kaikōmako are both trees that grow as divaricate shrubs as juveniles before producing the straighter trunks of mature trees.

MARINE LIFE

In New Zealand, marine life includes more than 1,000 types of seaweed, the most common and diverse of which are brown seaweeds, including kelp.[12] Kelp grows on rocky seafloors in massive stands referred to as kelp forests. These kelp forests provide hiding places and habitats for other sea life. They also affect the abundance or absence of light and how nutrients flow through the water.

Lemonwood trees have distinctive yellow-green leaves with a bright center stripe and curled edges.

Hector's dolphin is the rarest marine dolphin in the world. The World Wildlife Fund estimates that only 7,000 Hector's dolphins live in the wild.

Approximately half of the world's cetaceans, which include both whales and dolphins, can be found in New Zealand's waters.[13] The Hector's dolphin and a related subspecies called the Māui dolphin are found only in New Zealand. They are small dolphins, with the Hector's dolphin measuring five feet (1.5 m) long and the Māui dolphin measuring 5.3 feet (1.6 m) long. These dolphins may live in groups of up to 20 animals, but small groups of two to four animals are more common.[14] They eat many different things, including crustaceans, small fish, and cephalopods such as squid.

SEAMOUNTS

A seamount is an underwater mountain, and hundreds can be found in the waters of New Zealand. The majority are too deep in the ocean to have been explored. East of New Zealand, there is an area of ocean floor known as Chatham Rise where seamounts are host to *Solenosmilia variabilis* and *Madrepora oculata,* two species of stony coral. These corals form extensive habitats where a variety of other organisms live, including brittle stars, bristle worms, and squat lobsters. Volcanic seamounts north of North Island host some life-forms, but the lava there does not provide places for a diverse range of species to attach and find homes.

More species of the nation's 1,400 marine fish can be found around North Island than South Island because of North Island's warmer water.[15] Fish that live in these warm waters include mullets, snappers, and goatfish. The waters around South Island are cooler and provide homes for red and black cod as well as barracouta. New Zealand's unique fish include the largest seahorse species in the world, the big-belly seahorse. The male seahorse keeps the eggs of its young in a special pouch until these eggs hatch and tiny seahorses emerge. Another unique fish is the leatherjacket. Its skin looks rough and leathery. The leatherjacket also has a dorsal spine that it can retract.

New Zealand is also home to 1,500 species of sponges, including carnivorous sponges that are often found only in deep waters. Vast numbers of other species, including 1,100 species of anemone, jellyfish, and rocky or hard-bodied coral; 600 species of sea stars and other spiny animals; and 3,600 species of mollusks also thrive around New Zealand.[16] These marine animals

Large lion's mane jellyfish are frequently seen near Great Barrier Island off the coast of North Island.

live among a variety of aquatic features such as steep seamounts, or underwater mountains. They are also found near volcanoes, canyons, hydrothermal vents that release mineral-laden water into the ocean, and methane seeps, where methane gas escapes through a narrow crack in Earth's crust and into the water.

New Zealand is home to such a wide range of marine biodiversity because of the currents that surround its many islands. A band of warm water flows near Australia and around New Zealand's North and South Islands. Currents from just north of Antarctica bring in icy waters. These currents mix in different concentrations, creating bands that vary in temperature. That is why people can visit elephant seals in the cold waters of Fiordland and swim with sea turtles in the subtropical waters surrounding Poor Knights Islands.

CHAPTER **FOUR**

HISTORY

In the search to discover when people first arrived in what is now New Zealand, archaeologist Magdalena Bunbury used radiocarbon dating techniques to test the age of early settlements. Carbon-14 is a radioactive element that decays over time. Scientists can study the amount of carbon-14 present to determine the age of artifacts made from materials such as wood, bone, charred foods, and human remains.

In 2022 Bunbury reported that her analysis of moa eggshells, rat bones, and gnawed seeds from 436 archaeological sites shows that North Island was settled between 1250 and 1275. Humans reached South Island between 1280 and 1295.[1] The first people to arrive in New Zealand are now called the Māori.

Historians believe the first people who voyaged to New Zealand took canoes, likely equipped with sails and two hulls. The Māori people call their traditional canoes *waka*.

Māori legend says that Kupe, their ancestor, used stars and ocean currents to guide his voyaging canoe to New Zealand. According to this legend, he journeyed there from Hawaiki about 1,000 years ago.[2] Hawaiki is not on any modern map, but scientists believe that the Māori came from one or more Polynesian islands.

These first arrivals lived near the coasts in villages and fed themselves by fishing, hunting moa and other birds, and growing a limited number of crops. They brought the plants they grew with them when coming to New Zealand, including yam, a type of sweet potato called kumara, and taro. Taro is a plant that grows large, starchy underground stems called corms. In addition to the foods they planted, the Māori also gathered wild foods that grew in the area, including ferns, vines, palms, fungi, berries, fruits, and seeds.

After establishing themselves in the area, the Māori people moved inland, building villages where fence-like stockades and trenches helped protect the settlements. Warriors carried spear-like *taiaha* and club-like *mere* to further protect their homes. At this time, the Māori grew even more food in their gardens. This is also when stone and bone tools became more common.

MĀORI ORGANIZATION

Māori people who are descended from a common ancestor form a group, known as an *iwi*, that is led by an ariki. An iwi is divided up into numerous hapū, or groups of related people who own and farm land together. In 1857, under the threat of colonization, the Māori in the Waikato region of North Island elected a king, Te Wherowhero, who reigned as Pōtatua I. The Māori's hope was that a single leader could reduce warfare between iwi and help them resist European colonists.

THE EUROPEANS

Dutch explorer Abel Tasman had been sent to discover what he called a Great Southern Continent when he spotted the western coast of South Island in December 1642. He may have been the first European to see New Zealand. When a party from his ship attempted to land, they clashed at sea with the local Māori, who killed several of Tasman's men. The remainder of the Dutch party returned to the ship without reaching shore. Despite never setting foot on the island, Tasman claimed the land for Holland, calling it *Staten Landt*.

The next European credited with sighting New Zealand was Englishman Captain James Cook. Cook had sailed to Tahiti, an island in Oceania, to make astronomical observations in 1769. While sailing south, a member of Cook's crew spotted land. The ship sailed around the two main islands, allowing Cook to create a basic map of New Zealand.

The majority of Europeans who journeyed to New Zealand after Cook were there to make money. These included sealers who hunted seal and collected their skins, people who harvested lumber, and people who gathered New Zealand flax. Australian companies set up small settlements for whaling in New Zealand's bays. The town of Kororāreka, now called Russell, became a stopping place for deep-sea whaling ships from the United States, Britain, and France. Traders brought in supplies for the whalers, and Māori came to the area to purchase goods with their own items.

Missionaries moved among the Māori as well, working to convert them to Christianity. These Europeans brought more than new beliefs; they also carried diseases that were introduced to the

A statue of James Cook stands in Christchurch, New Zealand.

Māori, who had never developed a resistance to them. Among these new diseases were influenza or flu, tuberculosis, and the sexually transmitted infections syphilis and gonorrhea. When an epidemic killed large numbers of Māori, they called it a *tokotoko rangi*, or "spear from heaven."

COLONIZATION

In 1838, officials from Britain began efforts to take control of New Zealand. William Hobson, a naval officer, came to the area to act as lieutenant governor and counsel to the ariki, or Māori leaders. Since his representative found no Māori on South Island, Hobson said the British had discovered the island and claimed it as their own. The ariki on North Island signed the Treaty of Waitangi with Hobson, which they believed would solidify their leadership.

The Treaty of Waitangi was written in English and the Māori language, and this translation led

TUBERCULOSIS

Tuberculosis is a disease that is caused by bacteria. Tuberculosis spreads when groups of people gather and an infected person coughs or sneezes. Tuberculosis damages a person's lungs, making it harder for them to breathe and causing them to cough up blood. Today it can be treated with medication, but this treatment was not widely available until the 1950s and is still expensive and difficult to access in many places around the world. Earlier cases of tuberculosis were especially deadly to Māori, many of whom didn't get enough to eat and lived in crowded homes where the disease easily spread.

to differences in understanding between the two groups. The Māori version stated that the people gave up *kāwanatanga*. The British translated this word as "sovereignty" and said that the Māori had given up independence. In return, the Māori would be protected and guaranteed possession of their lands, which they could sell to Britain. However, the Māori meaning of *kāwanatanga* is more similar to "governance." Māori people interpreted the treaty to mean that the British—and later the New Zealand government—should be held responsible for the Māori people's well-being.

Initially New Zealand was part of the Colony of New South Wales, which is now an Australian state. New Zealand became a separate colony in 1841. Throughout this early colonial period, immigrants from England arrived in the colony and used sometimes-deceitful methods to push the Māori off their land. Disputes over land led to open warfare between colonists and Māori on North Island.

These struggles, known as the New Zealand Wars, began in the 1840s and lasted until the 1870s. Throughout the fighting, colonists and the British military tried to clear Māori people off their land so that it could be made available to colonists. Some Māori leaders fought alongside

Britain seized about 3,900 square miles (10,100 sq km) of Māori land during the New Zealand Wars.[4]

the British, believing that this was the best way to protect their own land. Māori leaders who fought against the British eventually lost the wars along with their lands. The New Zealand government estimates that approximately 560 British and colonial soldiers, 250 Māori fighting alongside the Europeans, and 2,000 Māori fighting against the British died in the conflict.[3]

BECOMING A NATION

During the New Zealand Wars, Britain passed the New Zealand Constitution Act in 1852. This law set up six provinces, each to be governed by an elected council. Eligible voters were men 21 years or older who owned or leased a specific amount of land. Although Māori were not specifically excluded, most Māori owned land as a group, and only people who owned or leased land individually were eligible to vote. The main elected official of each province was called a superintendent.

It was also during this time that New Zealand's gold rushes occurred. On May 23, 1861, Gabriel Read discovered gold in a valley in Otago Province on South Island. Soon after, thousands of men poured into the area, eager to find gold and achieve wealth. This gold rush not only temporarily increased the local population but also brought prosperity as bankers, merchants, farmers, and land sellers made money off these new arrivals. After this rush peaked in the mid-1860s, miners chased another major gold discovery on the west coast.

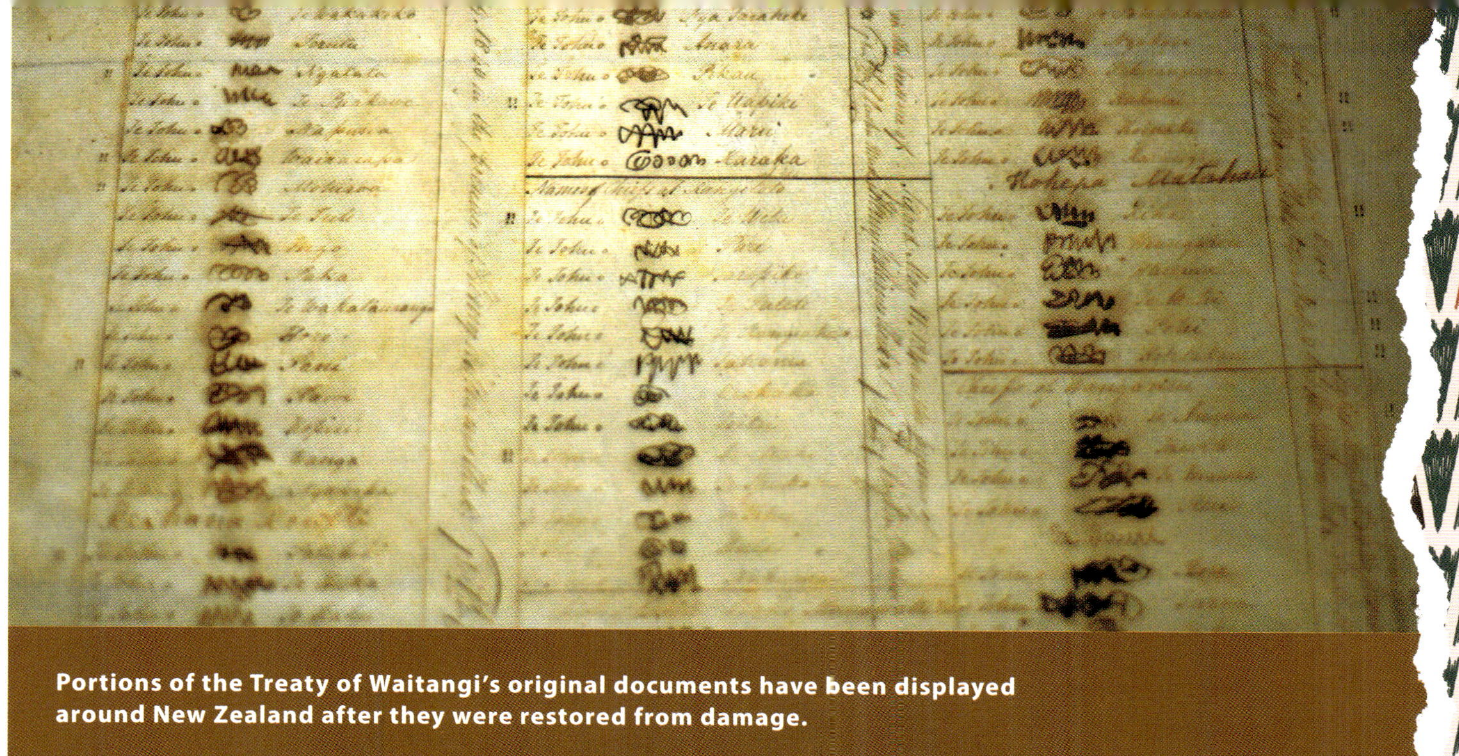

Portions of the Treaty of Waitangi's original documents have been displayed around New Zealand after they were restored from damage.

Other provincial governments saw Otago's prosperity and wanted something similar for their area. Governments borrowed money from overseas to try to achieve similar growth, but none of their plans worked. Faced with loans to pay back, provincial governments demanded that the central government help improve their economic situation and create opportunities for economic growth.

Julius Vogel was the colonial treasurer and believed that New Zealand's abundant resources could provide prosperity. Through the 1870s, he borrowed money to help bring over immigrants and build infrastructure such as roads, railroads, and telegraph lines. But when the overseas price fell for wool and wheat, two of New Zealand's major exports, so did the New Zealand

Magazine illustrations show New Zealand's gold miners in the 1860s.

government's income from taxes. The government's debts were larger than its income, leading to an economic depression and widespread unemployment that lasted until 1895.

The country's economy began to turn around under the Liberal government that took power in 1891. Prime Minister John Ballance, who was in office until his death in 1893, helped strengthen this government and its plans for change. Under Ballance, the government bought land from the

Māori, gave credit for leaseholders to rent this land long-term from the government, and built roads. Farming infrastructure for dairy and meat production grew on North Island during this time.

By the late 1800s, most New Zealanders of European descent had been born in New Zealand, which meant they didn't think of Britain as home. During World War I (1914–1918), New Zealanders fought alongside the British and proved themselves to be skilled soldiers. This promoted national pride and identity. In World War II (1939–1945), New Zealanders again fought alongside the United Kingdom in the European theater of the war until their own country was threatened by Japan. Then New Zealand acted independently from the United Kingdom and changed its focus to the fighting in the Pacific.

New Zealand became an independent nation in 1947. The Constitution Act 1986, which went into effect in 1987, formalized the country's system of government. It clarified the role of the monarch of the United Kingdom, who retained the role of head of state in New Zealand. Although the country is a constitutional monarchy, the monarch's role is largely ceremonial, and New Zealand is not part of the United Kingdom.

THE CHANGING FACE OF NEW ZEALAND

Throughout the 1970s and 1980s, the Māori people became more politically active. This led to the 1975 Treaty of Waitangi Act, which established a court of justice to investigate claims that the United Kingdom had failed to protect the Māori as required by the original treaty. A 1985 amendment to the act expanded investigations to include not only modern claims but also historical claims. Because of these investigations, in the early 1990s the government began granting the Māori financial, land, and resource compensation for past injustices.

In one 1998 case, South Island's Ngāi Tahu people signed a Deed of Settlement that detailed the compensation the Ngāi Tahu would receive. Valued at $170 million, it included the right to manage resources found on their lands as well as their sacred mountain.[5] Although this mountain was later gifted back to the nation, the settlement legally recognized the ties that the Māori people had to specific geographic regions. The act also led the government to apologize for suffering and injustice perpetrated against the Māori people.

In the late 1900s and early 2000s, New Zealand became a more diverse nation. A points-based immigration system rated applicants to enter the nation on skills, education, age, employment offers, and qualifications. This made it easier for many

EARTHQUAKE!

In September 2010, a major earthquake struck Christchurch, New Zealand. There were no fatalities, but the city suffered extensive damage to buildings and infrastructure. This was in part because the earthquake was centered about 28 miles (45 km) west of the city in the Canterbury Plains.[6] The plains were formed of gravel and sand deposits from ancient rivers. During the earthquake, the gravel and sandy soil began to move like water, intensifying the motion of the ground. This movement compressed the soil, which caused fountains of mud to shoot from the ground. Several mud fountains shot up in and around Christchurch during the earthquake, adding to the damage caused by the movement of the city's loose soil.

people to quickly qualify for residency. There was also a change in where immigrants came from, shifting from primarily the United Kingdom to Taiwan, China, and South Korea.

On February 26, 2020, health care officials reported the first case of COVID-19 in New Zealand. One month later, there were 100 reported cases, and Prime Minister Jacinda Ardern decided that the country wouldn't take any chances.[7] The government said that most people entering New Zealand from abroad would have to isolate themselves from other people for two weeks. Then one week later, the government announced a lockdown that closed business. Although the country briefly lifted its lockdown, it closed once more when cases soared. New Zealand slowly lifted its COVID-19 precautions during the following months.

By March 16, 2023, a total of 2,550 New Zealanders had died of COVID-19. That was nearly 53 out of every 100,000 people in the country's population. This rate was lower than that in many other countries. In comparison, 341 out of every 100,000 people in the United States died from COVID-19 during the same period.[8]

CHAPTER **FIVE**

PEOPLE AND CULTURE

New Zealand has a population of more than five million people, with most living on North Island. If the population were spread evenly across the country, 51 people would live in each square mile, or 20 people would live in each square kilometer.[1] This is lower than the population density of the United States, meaning that on average, people are more spread out in New Zealand. However, the actual population density varies within any country, with more people living in cities and urban areas.

The two largest cities in New Zealand are Auckland, with 1.63 million residents, and the nation's capital, Wellington, with 422,000 residents.[2] Christchurch, Manukau City, and North Shore are other major

Christchurch, New Zealand, is a growing city that brings together beautiful natural landscapes and an accessible city center.

population centers. Of New Zealand's five largest cities, only Christchurch is on South Island.

In 2023, 83.3 percent of New Zealand's population lived in the nation's cities.[4]

ANCESTRY AND CULTURE

New Zealanders have ancestry from all around the world, although European and Māori backgrounds are most common. Approximately 68 percent of New Zealand's population has European ancestry, 18 percent has Māori ancestry, 17 percent has Asian ancestry, 9 percent are descended from other Pacific peoples, and 2 percent has Latin American, African, or Middle Eastern ancestry.[3] People may identify with more than one category of ancestry.

New Zealand is considered a bicultural nation, with an equal presence of traditionally British and Māori customs. However, this wasn't always the case. It wasn't until the 1970s that Māori efforts to push back against the saturation of British culture began to see success. For example, in 1987, the Māori language became one of New Zealand's official languages, along with English and New Zealand Sign Language.

The Treaty of Waitangi supports official government recognition of Māori culture. But today, a great variety of people continue immigrating to New Zealand. Some people wonder whether the country should be seen not as bicultural but as multicultural. This would mean that the New Zealand government would officially make efforts to recognize the customs and rights of other cultures.

EMIGRANTS

Immigration takes place when people move into a country, and emigration is when people move out of a country. According to economists, New Zealanders may be moving to Australia, the United Kingdom, and other countries for job opportunities and a lower cost of living. Australia has been actively recruiting in New Zealand, looking for nurses, teachers, and police officers. New Zealanders do not need government approval through a visa to work in Australia, so it is easy for professionals to move from one country to the other.

RELIGION

More than 48 percent of New Zealanders do not practice any religion. Of those who do, the largest group are Christian, representing about 37 percent of the population. Ten percent of those are practicing Catholics.[5] Christians in New Zealand celebrate Christmas by decorating their homes and churches, but they also have barbecues and spend time outdoors. Easter is also celebrated but without the emphasis on springtime that is found in the United States and Europe, since the holiday occurs in winter. Chocolate eggs and Easter eggs are part of Easter celebrations in New Zealand.

After Christianity, the largest religious group is Hinduism at 2.7 percent of the population.[6] Hindu people have lived in New Zealand since the early 1800s. There are many medical, legal, and commercial professionals among New Zealand's Hindu community. The calendar of Hindu holidays includes Holi, the springtime harvest festival, and Diwali, the festival of lights. Diwali celebrations take place in Auckland and Wellington and include food, dancing, and music.

About 1.3 percent of New Zealand's population is Muslim.[7] The first Muslim immigrants to New Zealand arrived during the gold rushes in the 1800s. More Muslim immigrants arrived after 2000,

Tāmoko are traditional Māori tattoos. The practice dates back centuries. These tattoos can represent a person's history, family, and character.

ANTI-MUSLIM VIOLENCE

New Zealand's Muslims have been the victims of abuse and assault. In 2019, a gunman from Australia killed 51 Muslims and injured 49 more in two Christchurch mosques.[9] To honor the fallen, when Parliament met following the attacks, religious leaders from various faiths joined the procession entering the chamber. The session's traditional opening prayer was delivered in Arabic.

when immigration restrictions were reduced and refugees fled from conflict zones. In major cities and towns across New Zealand, there are mosques where Muslims worship. Islamic holidays are publicly celebrated, including Eid al-Fitr, the feast that marks the end of the annual fasting month of Ramadan. In 2002, Ashraf Choudhary became the first Muslim member of New Zealand's parliament.

Approximately another 1.3 percent of New Zealand's population practices the Māori religion.[8] Māori believe in mana, or a spiritual essence that is part of people, animals, land, and even objects. To maintain mana, people need to keep up a connection to other people and to the land. This is why the Māori's connection to their ancestral lands is critical.

HOLIDAYS

New Zealanders celebrate a variety of additional holidays, including many that are unique to this region and country. Each year on February 6, New Zealand celebrates Waitangi Day, remembering the signing of the Treaty of Waitangi in 1840. Waitangi Day was first celebrated in 1934 and has been a national holiday since 1974. The Waitangi Day Festival is held each year at the Treaty

Grounds, where the original treaty was signed. The celebration includes sports, craft stalls, food, and Māori dancing.

Anzac Day is observed on April 25 each year and commemorates the troops from the Australia and New Zealand Army Corps (ANZAC) who died in World War I's Gallipoli campaign, which was fought on the Gallipoli peninsula of Turkey in 1915. The Gallipoli campaign was fought between Turkish troops and troops from the United Kingdom, France, Australia, and New Zealand, whose goal was to weaken Turkey and ensure that ships could get to Russia. Among the dead were 2,779 New Zealanders, one-sixth of the New Zealand soldiers present.[10] On this holiday, people lay floral wreaths on graves and memorials, flags fly at half-mast, and remembrance ceremonies honor the fallen.

Matariki Day is the beginning of the Māori New Year and has been a national holiday since 2022. *Matariki* is the Māori name of a seasonal cluster of stars called the Pleiades or the Seven Sisters, and Matariki Day is the day this star cluster can first be seen, which varies from May to June each year on the Western calendar. The exact day of the holiday moves between those months. On this day, Māori people gather to remember loved ones who have died since Matariki last rose, give thanks for what they have, and look forward to the coming year.

LEISURE

A wide variety of foods are popular in New Zealand. Some are traditional British foods such as fish and chips, which is fried fish and French fries. Two dishes that are also popular in New Zealand are roast lamb and meat pies. Hangi pies are a type of meat pie cooked underground in a traditional Māori earth oven.

Māori food is popular in New Zealand. Some of the most common dishes are seafoods. These include pāua, or a type of mollusk called abalone; *tio*, or oysters; *kūtai*, or green-lipped mussels; and *kōura*, or freshwater crayfish.

Other foods come from the fields and forests of New Zealand, an area known as the bush. Popular bush foods include greens such as *pikopiko*, which are shoots from edible fern and watercress, and *kōwhitiwhiti*, which grows in freshwater rivers and creeks. Pūhā, or thistle, is served cooked with pork. The leaves of kawakawa trees are ground as a seasoning used to flavor other foods. Other bush foods are harakeke, or flax, which is used for cooking, and mānuka honey, which is made by bees that visit mānuka tree flowers.

Cooking food using geothermal heat is a traditional Māori cooking technique. Modern methods include cooking corn in geothermal pools.

Another popular food tradition is barbecue. New Zealanders cook lamb, beef, poultry, and sausages on the grill. Side dishes include potato salads, vegetable salads, and garlic bread.

New Zealanders also enjoy taking part in sports and outdoor activities such as mountain biking and trail running, which people do on hiking trails throughout the country. In cold weather they ski and snowboard. When near water, many New Zealanders surf, kayak, and sail.

Professional sports are popular too. When New Zealanders cheer on their favorite teams, they may be cheering for the Silver Ferns, which is the women's netball team. Netball is similar to basketball, although players do not dribble the ball and there is no backboard on the net. Another popular sport is cricket, which the British introduced to New Zealand. In cricket, two teams face off, with the batter from one team trying to score points by hitting the ball pitched by the other team's bowler. Many New Zealanders watch or play rugby. In this sport, two teams face off and attempt to reach the opponent's goal line while preventing the opposite team from doing the same.

SCORING IN RUGBY

A rugby team can earn points in two different ways. The first way is to score a try, which happens when a team gets the ball over the other team's goal line. This earns five points and a chance to convert the try and earn two additional points. To do this, the kicker must kick the ball through the uprights on the goalpost, similar to scoring a field goal in American football. The second way to score is during a penalty kick. If a team commits an infraction, the other team gets a chance to earn three points by kicking the ball through the goalposts.

ARTS

Music is an important art in New Zealand, with bands influenced by many types of music including jazz, reggae, blues, hip-hop, and rock and roll. Popular New Zealand musicians and bands include Crowded House, Lorde, and Six60. Local and international artists play at the Rhythm and Vines music festival, one of several festivals that takes advantage of the good weather from December through February. New Zealand also has a national symphony orchestra that performs in Wellington, Auckland, Christchurch, and even internationally.

New Zealand is home to a wide variety of visual artists too. Painting is a popular New Zealand art, and Charles Frederick Goldie is one of the country's most well-known painters. He worked in the late 1800s and early 1900s and is best known for his paintings of important Māori figures. Ola Höglund and Marie Simberg-Höglund are a well-known husband-and-wife team who create glass art including jewelry, vases, platters and more. Their work has appeared in more than 40 international exhibits and at the 2000 Olympic Games in Sydney, Australia.[11]

Māori arts include weaving and carving. The most frequently used weaving material is the harakeke flax plant. Traditionally, women used this material to create practical items such as *korowai*, or cloaks; *kete*, or baskets; and *whāriki*, or mats. Māori people continue to weave these items and others today. The Māori saying "Marry the woman who is always at the flax bush" shows how weavers are valued for their skill and hard work.[12]

Māori carve a variety of materials. Wood carving was used to create canoes for their ocean journeys. Bone and whale ivory were carved into fishhooks and ornaments for people to wear.

People can take tours of *Lord of the Rings* movie sets at Hobbiton.

Greenstone is still carved into necklace pendants, earrings, and decorative haircombs.

New Zealand is also known for filmmaking, especially the *Lord of the Rings* trilogy. International funding paid for these movies, which were filmed in New Zealand by Peter Jackson and his crew and released in the early 2000s. Jackson used local crews who helped build sets, film scenes, and manage props. Hobbiton, a location in the films, was built in New Zealand and continues to be a popular tourist attraction.

Another important figure in New Zealand film is Taika Waititi, who is a director, producer, screenwriter, and actor. He has been nominated for a variety of Emmy and Academy awards. Waititi won the 2020 Academy Award for Best Adapted Screenplay for *Jojo Rabbit*.

CHAPTER **SIX**

POLITICS

New Zealand has a parliamentary form of government loosely based on that of the United Kingdom. Parliament has one house chamber called the House of Representatives. This body has legislative power. As the legislative branch of the New Zealand government, Parliament makes and updates laws. It oversees taxes and how the government spends this money. It makes sure the government is doing what it should for the population. Members of Parliament, also known as MPs, are elected for three-year terms.

When electing MPs, New Zealanders get two votes. One vote is called the electorate vote, which citizens use to choose the specific candidate they want to represent their region. In each region, the candidate with the most votes wins and becomes an MP.

New Zealanders commonly call one of the parliament buildings in Wellington the Beehive due to its shape.

These are called electorate MPs. There are 65 general electorate MPs and seven Māori electorates in Parliament, for 72 total electorates. However, there are usually 120 seats available in all. The remaining seats are assigned based on the party vote.

The party vote is New Zealanders' second vote, where citizens choose the political party they want to represent them. This vote decides how many total MPs from each party are in Parliament. To be represented in Parliament, a political party must win one electorate in the first vote or get more than 5 percent of the party vote in the second vote. A party receives about the same percentage of seats in Parliament as the percentage of votes it won in the party election. For example, if a party wins 30 percent of the party vote, this party will have about 30 percent of the seats in Parliament.

Every electorate MP gets a seat in Parliament, but parties may have won more seats in the party vote than they won electorates. In this case, additional seats are filled based on party lists. These are lists each party creates before the election by making a ranked list of their candidates.

Normally there are 120 MPs, but a situation called an overhang may occur. If the formula used to allot seats states that a party should have fewer MPs than their party won electorates, all elected MPs keep their seats, resulting in more total MPs. An overhang occurred in 2023, when 123 MPs won seats in Parliament because three more electorates won seats than their parties were allotted.[1]

The party that wins the most parliamentary seats controls the executive branch of the government that term. The role of the executive branch is to administer the laws made by the legislative branch. The head of the winning party becomes the prime minister. The prime minister helps decide which MPs become ministers. Ministers oversee the work of government groups called ministries, which run various departments of government. A single minister may be a part of several ministries.

The prime minister also selects ministers to form the cabinet. The cabinet is the group with the highest level of power in the government. The cabinet approves laws and decides how the government spends money to achieve its goals.

The Ministry of Justice presides over New Zealand's court system. The courts enforce criminal law, settle lawsuits, protect people's rights, and make certain that the government works within the law. Most towns and cities have a district court. Above the district courts is the High Court, which hears serious criminal cases or cases where there is a large amount of money in dispute. Next are the Court of Appeal and the Supreme Court. The Court of Appeal reviews cases that were heard in lower

HANA-RAWHITI MAIPI-CLARKE

In 2023, when 21-year-old Hana-Rawhiti Maipi-Clarke was elected, she became the second-youngest elected MP. She opened her first speech with a haka, a type of Māori dance. Maipi-Clarke comes from a politically active family, although she had no previous political experience when she was elected. On what it means to be a Māori MP, she said, "We look after our land, we look after our people, we look after our culture and our language. We will always look after ourselves and everything surrounding us, so we will always look after others as well."[2]

courts if one party has challenged the result. The Supreme Court reviews cases of importance to the nation as a whole, such as cases that deal with the Treaty of Waitangi.

New Zealand's military is called the Defence Force, and it falls under the Ministry of Defence. Serving in the Defence Force is voluntary, and someone must be at least 17 years old to enlist. New Zealand's military is small. In 2024, approximately 4,300 people were in the country's army, 2,100 were in the navy, and 2,400 were in the air force.[3]

CONSTITUTIONAL MONARCHY

New Zealand is also a constitutional monarchy. Although New Zealand is not part of the United Kingdom, the Crown's monarch shares power with the New Zealand government. In 2022 this position passed from Elizabeth II to her son Charles III. In New Zealand, the monarch's role is largely symbolic.

The British monarch is represented in New Zealand by the governor-general, who holds this position for a five-year term. This person is selected by the monarch with recommendations from the New Zealand government. On October 21, 2021, Dame Cindy Kiro became the first Māori woman to hold the position of governor-general.

QUEEN ELIZABETH II

New Zealand's first visit by a reigning monarch came when Elizabeth II visited in 1953. There had been five previous royal visits, but these visits were made by the son or brother of the reigning monarch. In December, Queen Elizabeth and her husband, Philip, arrived in New Zealand and toured the country for almost six weeks. They visited 46 towns and cities, and an estimated 75 percent of New Zealanders came out to see the queen.[4]

MINI **BIO**

JACINDA ARDERN

Jacinda Ardern was born in Hamilton, New Zealand, and spent part of her childhood in the town of Murupara, where she saw barefoot children with little to eat. This experience was part of what inspired her to enter politics. In 1999 she joined the Labour Party. After graduating from the University of Waikato with a degree in politics and public relations, she became an adviser in the office of then prime minister Helen Clark. In 2005, Ardern went to London, the United Kingdom, and worked in the Government Cabinet Office of the UK prime minister at the time, Tony Blair. In 2007, Ardern was elected President of the International Union of Socialist Youth.

In 2008, Ardern entered New Zealand's parliament as a list candidate. She became the MP for the Auckland electorate Mount Albert in early 2017 and the leader of the Labour Party in August 2017. That year she became prime minister at the age of 37. She was the country's youngest prime minister and the world's youngest female head of government at that time. In 2023 Ardern was named Dame Grand Companion of the New Zealand Order of Merit, which is the country's second-highest honor.

Ardern resigned from her role as prime minister in 2023 after protests against her COVID-19 policies led to personal and professional challenges.

King Charles III, then the Prince of Wales, shared a traditional greeting with a Māori woman during his visit to New Zealand in 2015.

Within the constitutional government, the governor-general dissolves Parliament before an election and reconvenes it after the election. The governor-general also signs off on parliamentary bills, giving royal assent so the bills become law. The governor-general is often the person who travels around the world to represent New Zealand in official matters.

The governor-general is also a ceremonial and community figure. They host visiting dignitaries, hold banquets, attend military services, and give out medals and honors. The governor-general may visit groups as a public speaker and encourage people who are working for their communities.

POLITICAL PARTIES

Political parties play an important role in New Zealand politics. The nation's political parties create policies on various issues, such as employment and climate change, and inform voters about these policies. Yet before the late 1800s, there were no political parties in New Zealand, and all candidates in New Zealand's elections ran as independents.

Today, there are many parties in New Zealand. Each party has different policies. Six of these parties had members in Parliament in 2024. The Labour Party wants to be certain that New Zealand's services benefit all citizens while educating these same citizens about democratic socialism. When it was formed in 1916, this party pushed for government, rather than private, ownership of land and industry. The Green Party stands for social responsibility and recognizes that humans are part of and dependent on the natural world. This party first won a seat in Parliament in 1993. The National Party seeks to limit government influence while promoting business and the freedom of individuals.

The ACT Party, formerly called the Association of Consumers and Taxpayers, promotes active law enforcement, improving schools in disadvantaged areas, and cutting government spending. Te Pāti Māori supports the maintenance of the Waitangi Treaty, promotes cultural diversity, and aims to help all New Zealanders. The New Zealand First party seeks to improve the health and education of New Zealanders, shrink government

There are 17 political parties registered with the New Zealand Electoral Commission.[5]

Debbie Ngarewa-Packer was first elected to Parliament in 2020 as a member of the Te Pāti Māori party, of which she became co-leader.

and lower taxes, and develop an economy based on exports.

POLITICAL SYMBOLS

The New Zealand flag is navy blue with two important symbols. In the top left corner is a red-and-white Union Jack to represent the nation's connection, past and present, to the United Kingdom. On the right side, four red stars outlined in white represent the Southern Cross, one of the primary constellations visible in the night sky of the Southern Hemisphere.

Another flag that is sometimes displayed in the country is the National Māori Flag, also called *tino rangatiratanga*. This black, red, and white flag is an abstract representation of a *koru*, a fern's shoot. The white band in the center of the flag also symbolizes the Māori name for New Zealand, *Aotearoa*, which means "the land of the long white cloud."

THE NATIONAL FLAG REFERENDUM

Since Australia's flag also has a Union Jack and stars, New Zealand's parliament worked to replace the New Zealand flag with something more distinct from Australia's. A contest in 2015 and 2016 brought in thousands of entries, and many of the designs included ferns or a red mountain. One submission even showed a kiwi bird with lasers coming from its eyes. In the end, the public decided to keep the original New Zealand flag, although a few of the entries are sometimes seen at athletic events.

New Zealand's national colors are black, white or silver, and red ocher. New Zealand's athletic teams frequently wear black and white or silver, with their names reflecting these colors. New Zealand's rugby union team is the All Blacks, the All Whites are the men's soccer team, and the Black Sticks are the women's hockey team.

The New Zealand coat of arms can be used only by the New Zealand government. A European woman and a Māori ariki flank the central shield. A sheep, a sheaf of wheat, and hammers emphasize the importance of agriculture and mining. Ferns splay out below the shield.

New Zealand has two national anthems. The first anthem is "God Save the King," which is played whenever a member of the royal household is present. This anthem has been a part of New Zealand's identity since British colonists settled in the area. The poem "God Defend New Zealand" was originally put to music in 1876. In 1977, it was named as the second national anthem of New Zealand.

CHAPTER **SEVEN**

ECONOMICS

New Zealand had a gross domestic product (GDP) of more than $254 billion in 2023. GDP measures the value of the goods and services produced by a country. This amount was an increase of 0.6 percent from 2022. Overall, the country is ranked economically at number 68 out of 224 nations around the world based on GDP.[1]

New Zealand is a country rich in natural resources, including minerals. Mining began before European settlement, with Māori mining both argillite and greenstone. Argillite is a fine-grained rock made up of clay particles that settled and were covered by more layers, which generated a lot of pressure and heat, causing the particles to become stone. Argillite is an excellent stone for making tools or ornaments, and the Māori use it to create knifelike tools to prepare food

Gold mines and coal mines are New Zealand's largest mines.

and axe-like adzes. The Māori call the stone *pakohe* and mine it in the mountains or from boulders in streams. Argillite items are still made and sold today.

The Māori also mine greenstone, which is known in their language as *pounamu*. The geological name for the stone is nephrite, and it is found only on South Island. Māori artists still carve pounamu into jewelry and ornaments for Māori and for sale to tourists.

Modern mining includes the extraction of coal, with approximately 3.2 million short tons (2.9 million metric tons) extracted in 2021.[2] Coal mined at different locations has different qualities, and the New Zealand coal that is good for use in industrial furnaces, called bituminous coal, is exported for use in steel production in South Korea, Japan, India, and Australia. While renewable energy resources are being developed, coal is still used in New Zealand to generate electricity, produce steel, heat greenhouses for growing crops, and heat many public buildings.

ENVIRONMENTAL COSTS

There are environmental costs to mining. Surface mining, which is the type used to mine gold, tears up the ground, removing trees and other plants, whose roots hold the soil in place. When it rains, the soil that has been exposed is washed into waterways and becomes sediment, settling at the bottom of the waterways. This sediment muddies water, which can damage fish's gills and make it harder for fish to find food. Mines use the chemical cyanide in the mining process, which can be harmful since the substance is poisonous. Mines keep this toxic and highly acidic chemical in open ponds. If a dam breaks or the pond floods, this toxic water can run into streams and lakes where it kills wildlife. One of the primary government agencies that ensures damage is minimal and within legal limits is the Environmental Protection Authority.

New Zealand's black iron sand comes from volcanic activity more than two million years ago.

The black sand of New Zealand is known as iron sand. Approximately 1.3 million short tons (1.2 million metric tons) of iron sand is mined each year at the Waikato North Head deposit on North Island.[3] The sand is processed into metallic iron, which can then be cast into slabs and used to make a variety of products, including building materials.

Gold and silver are both mined in New Zealand, but the silver is often considered a byproduct of gold mining because it is less valuable. In 2022, 12,740 pounds (5,800 kg) of gold were mined in New Zealand.[4] The nation's largest mine is at Macraes Flat on South Island. New Zealand gold and silver are shaped into jewelry and used to make technology such as cell phones, televisions, and computer chips.

The most common type of mines are open pit mines. Creating these mines disrupts the natural landscape, but the area can be rehabilitated once the gold has been extracted. Mining companies save the topsoil excavated for the mine and use heavy machinery to recontour the landscape before putting the topsoil back into place. The area returns to pasture.

Stone is also quarried in New Zealand. Between 20 and 30 million years ago, shallow seas covered the nation. Shells and bone settled to the seafloor, forming limestone. Tectonic plates moved and created mountains of limestone. The mineral is now mined from the mountains. Much of the limestone quarried in New Zealand is crushed for use in roads and as fertilizer in agriculture.

Another stone that is quarried in New Zealand is pumice. This is a lightweight volcanic rock that can float. It is used as drainage material in construction sites and is also added to potting soils to help drain water.

Other minerals are also extracted in New Zealand. Clay is a type of thick, heavy soil that soaks up water. It is made of fine particles of weathered stone and can be found throughout New Zealand. When heated in a process called firing, clay becomes hard. New Zealand's clay is used to make fine porcelain dishes, rugged stoneware dishes, and bricks. Clay is also used both to form sheets of paper and to coat paper. Its absorbent qualities make it valuable for creating cat litter and processing oils, beer, and wine.

MĀORI FARMS

In 2022, Māori farms were approximately three times larger than non-Māori farms on average. This is because almost half of the Māori farms are managed by Māori authorities. These business collectives manage land owned by many Māori people. The authorities are responsible for the actual agriculture, selling the crops and livestock, distributing income, and paying taxes. Because of the larger farm size, they average three times as many beef cattle, five times as many dairy cattle, and seven times as many sheep compared with non-Māori farms. They also maintain more land as forest on average than other farms.[5]

AGRICULTURE AND INDUSTRY

Early in New Zealand's history, the country could be reached only by ship. This made it vital for early industry to manufacture the things the people in New Zealand required, as it was difficult to import goods into the country. In the 1800s, the nation's industry focused on manufacturing and repairing agricultural machinery, building ships, processing timber, and brewing. Agriculture is still important, and many modern New Zealand industries process agricultural goods.

New Zealand's farmers grow or raise a wide variety of agricultural products. Sheep, beef cattle, and dairy make up a large part of the livestock industry. Major crops include wine grapes, kiwi fruits, potatoes, apples, oats, wheat, barley, corn, peas, lentils, canola, and various types of clover.

New Zealand is one of the top exporters of wool in the world.

Australia is one of the leading export destinations for fresh New Zealand–grown fruits and vegetables.

There were approximately 25.1 million sheep in New Zealand in 2023.[7]

Much of New Zealand's industry involves the processing of meat, wool, and dairy before these products are exported to other countries. These dairy products include milk, milk powders, butter, cheese, and infant formula. Thousands of people work in New Zealand's dairy farming industry, and even more people are employed processing these dairy products. China, Australia, Indonesia, and the United States purchase most of New Zealand's dairy exports, which in 2023 were valued at nearly $16 billion.[6]

CURRENCY

New Zealand's currency is the New Zealand dollar, sometimes called the kiwi. It is printed in denominations of five dollars, ten dollars, $20, and $50. Coins are minted at ten cents, 20 cents, 50 cents, one dollar, and two dollars. The coins are named based on value, so what someone in the United States would call a dime, someone in New Zealand calls a ten-cent coin. The one-dollar and two-dollar coins replaced the one-dollar and two-dollar banknotes in 1990. One hundred New Zealand cents equal one New Zealand dollar.

New Zealand's bills are printed on a polymer because it is harder to counterfeit than paper, meaning that it is difficult for people to create fake money. This material is also sturdier than paper and can withstand going through a washing machine. Banknotes are printed in bright colors with

In 2024, one New Zealand dollar was worth approximately 61 cents in US currency.[11]

text in both English and Māori. Important people pictured on the banknotes include Edmund Hillary on the five-dollar note, Queen Elizabeth II on the $20 note, and Māori statesman Apirana Ngata on the $50 note.

INFRASTRUCTURE

Because of New Zealand's geography, people use a wide range of transportation, including flying or taking boats between islands and driving across North Island and South Island. New Zealand has one of the highest rates of car ownership in the world. About 115,800 used cars were imported to New Zealand in 2023, with the vast majority of these vehicles coming from Japan.[8] About two-thirds of the total miles of roads and highways are paved, and the rest are unsealed roads made of clay or loose gravel.[9]

Public transportation is also popular in New Zealand. Major cities have public bus systems and may have suburban railways. Ferries are another public transportation option available through Auckland Transport. For example, these boats take passengers across Hauraki Gulf on North Island.

Many people travel from island to island by plane, and there are 62 airports in New Zealand.[10] These include international airports that receive flights from other countries, smaller domestic airports, private airports, and military airports. The three international airlines based in New Zealand are Air Chathams, Air New Zealand, and Airwork.

Infrastructure involves not only the roads that get people from place to place but also the systems that generate energy. New Zealand is striving for more renewable energy usage each year. Renewable energy sources can continue to produce energy without being used up, unlike coal or fossil fuels that are limited resources. In 2022 renewable energy made up 30 percent of the total energy used in the nation.[12] Renewable energy in New Zealand includes electricity generated by wind power, solar power, and waterpower. There is also renewable energy that is used directly instead of being harnessed to generate electricity, such as the use of geothermal energy, or heat from within Earth, as a heat source. The primary nonrenewable means of generating electricity include the burning of coal, natural gas, and oil.

SUSTAINABLE INDUSTRY

Carbon dioxide is one of the main gases causing climate change. It is released when fossil fuels such as coal and gasoline are burned. Trees contain carbon, so deforestation also releases gas that contributes to climate change. The New Zealand government is working to reduce and offset the nation's carbon emissions. Programs that offset emissions take actions to naturally reduce carbon dioxide in the atmosphere. Their aim is to balance out the emissions of other necessary processes. In 2018 the New Zealand government announced One Billion Trees. This program aims to offset carbon emissions by planting trees in New Zealand. Between 2018 and 2024, the program paid for nearly 700 million trees to be planted.[13]

CHAPTER **EIGHT**

NEW ZEALAND TODAY

Life varies around New Zealand. In the morning, a typical breakfast may be cereal, toast and sliced tomato, or a smoothie. People who want a hot breakfast might select French toast, scrambled or fried eggs, or porridge made from oats boiled in water. On school days, younger children eat a midmorning snack they bring from home, and then they have lunch, which might be a sandwich, fruit, raw vegetables, and a dessert item such as a muffin, cookie (which New Zealanders call a biscuit), or scone.

Many New Zealanders are physically active. Young people frequently attend extracurricular activities.

New Zealanders often enjoy the outdoors and explore natural wonders such as Tongariro National Park.

Rugby is one of the most popular sports for secondary school students to play in New Zealand.

These may include ballet, swimming, gymnastics, sports teams, or Scouts, an organization for young people that gives them opportunities to learn about and explore nature. Music lessons are also popular.

Families are also active outdoors, often swimming at a lake, taking a dog for a walk, riding a bike, or walking the neighborhood to get a treat such as coffee or ice cream. If the weather is nice, family dinners may be eaten outside. Some common options include take-out fish and chips; sausages, grilled potatoes, and salad; burritos; homemade pizza; or prawn and vegetable wraps.

Rugby is considered the national sport, and New Zealanders have been working to revive it following the COVID-19 lockdowns that disrupted community sports. November 2023 was the end of the first regular year of play since the lockdowns, and the season saw increased participation. New Zealand continues pushing to bring in more players. Children start out playing RipRugby. This is a version of the game in which rips, or flags, are carried by each player for opponents to tear off instead of tackling.

In the early to mid-2020s, more women and girls began playing the sport. Between 2022 and 2023,

HEADFIRST

Olympic gold medalist and Black Fern player Ruby Tui is a spokesperson for HeadFirst, New Zealand Rugby's initiative to promote mental health. This initiative encourages rugby players to take small steps toward caring for their mental health, such as checking in with people they trust and sharing their struggles. Tui said, "Knowing the importance of looking after our mental well-being is a great start, but in order to have a real impact within our rugby community, we need to combine that with simple and practical steps everyone can take to help both themselves and others."[1]

At the 2022 Women's Rugby World Cup, 150,000 fans attended 26 matches.[6]

there was a 20 percent rise in participation among that demographic.[2] Part of this enthusiasm among female players may have come from the fact that in 2022, New Zealand hosted the Women's Rugby World Cup. In the final game, the New Zealand Black Ferns defeated England's Red Roses 34 to 31 to win the cup. The Black Ferns have a win rate of about 85 percent.[3]

EDUCATION

In New Zealand, the school year is broken into four terms of ten weeks each. Term one usually runs from late January or early February to early or mid-April. Term two starts in late April and ends in late June or early July. Term three runs from mid-July to mid-September, and term four goes from early or mid-October to mid-December.

Early childhood education isn't required, but most children participate. In 2024, nearly 97 percent of young children were in early education programs.[4] These programs are for children from birth to six years of age. The government pays for up to six hours a day of early education.

There are different types of early childhood education programs in New Zealand. In teacher-led programs, including formal kindergartens and Montessori programs, half of the educators must be licensed teachers. Home-based education and care have a limit of four children.[5] In parent-led programs, also called whānau-led programs, a parent, extended family member, or caregiver is the teacher. Some parents choose to educate their children in the Māori language.

In New Zealand, students are required to attend school from ages six to 16. There are three tiers of education in New Zealand: primary schools, intermediate schools, and secondary schools. Primary schools are for children ages five to ten who are in year one to year six. Under the New Zealand National Curriculum, they study English, mathematics, the arts, science, social sciences, technology, health, and physical education.

Intermediate schools are for children ages 11 to 12 and in years seven and eight. Students continue in the New Zealand National Curriculum. Secondary schools are for children ages 13 to 18 and in years nine through 13. Schools continue the New Zealand National Curriculum but also prepare students for the National Certificate in Educational Achievement.

The National Certificate in Educational Achievement consists of three levels. Students take courses that meet different standards. The possible results include failing, achieving, achieving with merit, or achieving with excellence. Some standards, including English, math, and science, must be met by all students. But students may also choose standards related to jobs such as those in technology or hospitality.

By being able to select standards in areas where they excel, students are better able to show their strengths than with a single standardized test. When students pass a standard, they earn credits. Students must achieve 80 credits at that level to move up to the next level.[7]

Most primary, intermediate, and secondary schools are government funded and free for students to attend from ages five to 19. As an alternative to the New Zealand National Curriculum schools, students can enroll in *kura kaupapa* Māori schools, which are generally called kura.

Many schools in New Zealand require students to wear a uniform.

In these government-funded state schools, classes are taught in the Māori language. Classes emphasize the culture and values of the Māori.

About 10 percent of the students in New Zealand study in a state-integrated school, which also teaches the national curriculum but with a different focus or method of teaching.[8] These schools may be associated with a specific religion, such as Catholicism, or a specific method of education, such as Montessori or Waldorf. The actual school building and land is owned by the school, but the education is government funded. These schools charge tuition to maintain their facilities.

Less than 5 percent of New Zealand's students attend private schools. Some of these schools are coeducational, meaning there are both male and female students. Others are single-gender schools, and some are boarding schools, meaning that the students may live on school grounds during the school term. Tuition for the different types of private schools starts at about 25,000 New Zealand dollars per year.[9]

In New Zealand, parents can homeschool their children, but they must apply for a Ministry of Education Certificate of Exemption. To get this certificate, the parents must be able to show the government that their children will regularly attend classes. They also have to show that the education their children receive will be as good as what they would get at a state-registered school.

After high school, students can choose to attend trade schools, Wānanga, or university. At trade or vocational schools, New Zealand's students can study fields such as creative arts and design, travel and tourism, and construction. The goal for vocational and trade study in New Zealand is to learn something that helps the student find a job.

The Māori helped establish three Wānanga, which are university-level institutions that offer degrees through the PhD level. Wānanga education is open to any New Zealand resident and includes studies in Māori history and language as well as instruction in fields taught at other institutions. Part of what sets the Wānanga apart is the idea that students are part of a close community.

New Zealand also has eight state-funded universities where students can pursue degrees.[10] Seven offer education in topics ranging from archaeology to engineering and linguistics to veterinary science. One specializes in degrees related to agriculture.

CITIZEN WELL-BEING

One of the stated goals of the New Zealand government is to ensure the well-being of its citizens. The factor that New Zealand considers most strongly in judging well-being is the income of New Zealanders, but other factors are also important. In 2019, Prime Minister Jacinda Ardern introduced a budget to reduce domestic violence and child poverty and to improve housing opportunities. This meant prioritizing mental health and child well-being and preventing family violence.

Ardern made these decisions because, when compared with other nations in the Organisation for Economic Co-operation and Development (OECD), New Zealand struggled in terms of family violence and child poverty. The OECD is an organization of 38 nations working together to solve challenges. It uses the median income of each country to determine the poverty line. In each

TE WĀNANGA O AOTEAROA

Students who attend the Māori university Te Wānanga o Aotearoa can earn many degrees similar to those from other universities, such as forestry, money management, and education degrees. But there are also degrees that are unique to Wānanga education. These include a bachelor of Māori art and a master of applied Indigenous knowledge. In addition to degrees, students can learn more about being Māori, including studying the language and the culture. Wānanga acknowledges that study at a university may not be best for everyone and offers home-based distance learning as well.

In 2021, New Zealand's parliament passed legislation funding new housing development throughout the country. Building more homes can make housing less expensive and more accessible.

country, half the population makes more than the median income and half makes less. Households below the poverty line make less than half the median income of the total population.

In 2020, 14.8 percent of New Zealand's children lived below the poverty line. In the early 2020s, the highest poverty rate in the OECD was in Costa Rica at 28.5 percent, and the lowest was in Finland at 3 percent.[11] Across OECD countries, the average percentage of children living below the poverty line is about 13 percent.[12]

According to Maree Brown, director of the Child Wellbeing Unit in the Department of the Prime Minister and Cabinet in 2019, one way to address this issue is to talk to people at the community level. They are the ones who know what their people need to be well. Community-driven solutions may be more successful than those led only by the government.

The Māori people rank at the bottom of every indicator of well-being, including education, numbers in the prison population, and life expectancy. Māori people are at a lower socioeconomic status, meaning they make less money than other New Zealanders on average. This makes it harder for them to get the health care they need when sick, and the health care they do have access to is generally of lower quality. Māori activists want to change this, but the conservative government elected in 2022 following Ardern's Labour government wanted to review the Treaty of Waitangi and reduce or remove some of the treaty-based benefits received by the Māori. Reducing these benefits may lead to a further decline in Māori well-being.

In early December 2023, thousands of Māori protested about government plans to reduce Māori protections. Prime Minister Christopher Luxon didn't believe government services should be based on race, and he aimed to reverse Māori-specific governmental supports. One such example is the government-mandated quota for the number of Māori people accepted into New Zealand's medical schools, which aimed to address the disparity between Māori and non-Māori medical professionals in New Zealand.

Claire Charters spoke to the US media organization National Public Radio (NPR) about these protests and the importance of governmental support for the Māori. Charters is a professor of law at the University of Auckland, where she specializes in Indigenous peoples' rights. She is also a tribally appointed partner at the New Zealand Human Rights Commission. Charters's argument for preserving these programs is that the government has a responsibility to support Māori people because their lower rates of well-being are due to historic mistreatment. She said, "There's a very strong correlation between these sort of socioeconomic factors . . . and the experience of colonization. Now, that would suggest that certainly being Māori is something that you should take into account when trying to achieve equity and equality. What the government is proposing currently is something very different, namely that those factors of being indigenous are irrelevant."[13]

TOURISM'S IMPACT

Between 6 and 8 percent of New Zealand's workforce is employed in the tourism industry, and tourists bring in billions of dollars to the country each year.[14] Many tourists visit Māori sites and learn about this culture that is still

Some New Zealanders working in the tourism industry are tour guides. They lead trips and teach visitors about the location.

New Zealand's national parks provide important habitats for animals such as kea. Ensuring that these areas stay protected and clean is important for many species.

thriving today. Others hike, kayak, and explore New Zealand's national parks to see glaciers, beaches, and forests.

New Zealand has 13 national parks total, one of which is on Stewart Island. These parks encompass approximately 11,600 square miles (30,000 sq km).[15] They offer visitors the opportunity to take short walks, long hikes, and boat trips. People can even stay overnight in remote wilderness areas.

At Egmont National Park on North Island, visitors can take a hike to the top of Mount Egmont, also known as Taranaki Maunga, which is 8,261 feet (2,518 m) tall.[16] Visitors can also walk through rainforests. On South Island, Mount Aspiring National Park offers visitors the opportunity to walk through valleys gouged by glaciers.

Despite the benefits of tourism, New Zealanders also see its negative environmental impacts. Tourism contributes to carbon dioxide emissions, creates additional waste that ends up in landfills, and leads to crowds that can harm the natural landscape of previously isolated areas. Environmental impacts such as air and water pollution and waste are especially concerning to New Zealanders. The usage of water and energy brought about by tourism may also put a strain on New Zealand's natural resources.

Because of the negative impact tourism has on New Zealand's environment, some tourist destinations are moving toward sustainable tourism. An example of this movement is educational programs that teach tourists about the importance of New Zealand's plant and animal life. One of these programs is the Wairaurahiri jet boat tour. It combines the excitement of a powerful, high-speed boat with a trip into remote areas of Fiordland National Park, where tourists learn about the plants and animals that live there. Tourists learn about the need to protect animals from invasive predators. One way that the trip is made more environmentally friendly is that a minimum number of passengers must be in each boat, since boats with fewer passengers are less efficient. Visitors can also pay to sponsor a stoat trap to help remove predators from the local environment.

Other suggestions have been made about how to mitigate the impact of tourism. In 2019, New Zealand instituted an international tourist tax, a fee of 35 New Zealand dollars that tourists pay when they enter the country. Some of this money is put

MOTU KAIKŌURA

In 2003, Motu Kaikōura, an island near Auckland, became available for sale and the government of New Zealand bought it. New Zealand established the Motu Kaikōura Community Trust, which oversees researchers, volunteers, and educators working to conserve the island and return its original flora and fauna, such as the black petrel seabird. Conservationists began by removing the invasive animals and plants introduced during the long period when the island was commercially farmed. Visitors to the area can stay at the lodge and take part in maintenance, such as road construction, and environmental projects, such as removing non-native plants.

toward conservation and environmental efforts. In September 2024, the New Zealand government raised the fee to 100 New Zealand dollars to continue to offset demands placed on infrastructure by international visitors.[17]

Tama Potaka, the conservation minister elected in 2022, said that he is not against these kinds of fees. "If you put a value on experiences and you put limits around the number of people that can visit these places, you give people the sense that there needs to be a greater consideration. . . . [Visiting the area] is actually something you need to do mindfully rather than just do it as a way of ticking off that bucket list."[18] In this way, the government will help preserve New Zealand's natural wonders and way of life for both residents and visitors for many years to come.

As an island nation, New Zealand will continue to face the challenges and benefits of being geographically isolated. This isolation led to a unique culture and a land of diverse plants and animals found nowhere else. New Zealanders are also part of an increasingly global community. Their hopefulness about the future may be part of what enables them to look for ways to work with the changing environment while still inviting visitors to come experience the beautiful natural and cultural landscape of the country.

ESSENTIAL **FACTS**

OFFICIAL NAME: NEW ZEALAND

GEOGRAPHY

Area: 103,799 square miles (268,838 sq km)

Highest Elevation: Aoraki/Mount Cook at 12,218 feet (3,724 m)

Lowest Elevation: Pacific Ocean at 0 feet (0 m)

PEOPLE

Population: 5 million (2024 est.)

Most Populous City: Auckland (1.7 million)

Ethnic Groups: Primarily European, Māori, Asian, other Pacific Islanders, other

Religions: Christianity, Hinduism, Māori religion, Islam, Buddhism, other, none

GOVERNMENT

Type of Government: Parliamentary democracy under a constitutional monarchy

Capital: Wellington

Head of State: British monarch, represented by governor-general

Head of Government: Prime minister

Legislature: Unicameral House of Representatives, generally called Parliament

ECONOMY

Currency: New Zealand dollar

Major Industries: Agriculture, forestry, fishing, manufacturing, mining, construction, financial services, real estate, tourism

Natural Resources: Natural gas, iron ore, sand, coal, timber, hydropower, gold, limestone

NATIONAL SYMBOLS

National Anthem: "God Defend New Zealand," "God Save the King"

National Colors: Black, white, red ocher

National Coat of Arms: European woman and Māori man standing on either side of a blue, white, and red shield

GLOSSARY

biodiversity
The many different plants and animals in an ecosystem.

biome
A community of plants and animals that adapt to and live in a specific climate.

climate
The long-term weather pattern in an area.

colonization
The practice of gaining political control over another country, occupying it with settlers, and exploiting its resources.

democratic socialism
A set of political beliefs supporting a democratic transition from capitalism to socialism.

dorsal
Having to do with the back of a living thing.

habitat
The natural environment of an organism.

invasive
Describing non-native plants or animals that grow and spread, harming native species.

invertebrate
An animal without a spinal column.

mangrove
A shrub or tree with tangled roots that grows near the coast in tropical swamps that flood at high tide.

mantle
The layer of Earth between the core and the outer crust.

prawn
A marine crustacean that looks similar to a shrimp.

terrestrial
Living on or growing from land.

vascular plant
A plant that has special tissues that conduct water and minerals through the organism.

ADDITIONAL **RESOURCES**

SELECTED BIBLIOGRAPHY

Morell, Virginia. “Why Did New Zealand’s Moas Go Extinct?” *Science*, 17 Mar. 2014, science.org. Accessed 10 Sept. 2024.

“New Zealand.” *CIA World Factbook*, 1 Oct. 2024, cia.gov. Accessed 8 Oct. 2024.

“The Treaty in Practice.” *New Zealand History*, 5 Oct. 2021, nzhistory.govt.nz. Accessed 6 Sept. 2024.

FURTHER READINGS

Edwards, Sue Bradford. *Australia*. Abdo, 2023.

Experience New Zealand. Lonely Planet, 2022.

Mooney, Carla. *Climate Change*. Abdo, 2025.

ONLINE RESOURCES

To learn more about New Zealand, please visit **abdobooklinks.com** or scan this QR code. These links are routinely monitored and updated to provide the most current information available.

MORE INFORMATION

For more information on this subject, contact or visit the following organizations:

Archives New Zealand

10 Mulgrave St.
Wellington 6011
archives.govt.nz

Archives New Zealand contains information on immigration to the country, court documents, school records, and more. The archives' website has research guides to help students learn about different topics relevant to the country.

Department of Conservation

Conservation House, 18-32 Manners St.
Wellington 6011
doc.govt.nz

The Department of Conservation is responsible for protecting the plants and animals of New Zealand. It teaches about conservation and gives people a chance to help.

New Zealand Parliament

1 Molesworth St.
Pipitea, Wellington 6011
parliament.nz/en

In addition to passing laws to benefit New Zealand, Parliament educates people about how democracy works. People may visit Parliament to see where MPs work and make laws. The building also hosts a collection of art and other artifacts.

SOURCE **NOTES**

CHAPTER 1. A TOUR OF NEW ZEALAND

1. "The Gondwana Arboretum—Kauri." *YouTube*, uploaded by Auckland Botanic Gardens, 18 Sept. 2018, youtube.com. Accessed 8 Oct. 2024.
2. "International Travel: December 2023." *StatsNZ*, 15 Feb. 2024, stats.govt.nz. Accessed 8 Oct. 2024.
3. Warren Moran and Conrad Alexander Blyth. "New Zealand." *Britannica*, 8 Oct. 2024, britannica.com. Accessed 8 Oct. 2024.
4. "Countries of Australia and Oceania." *Nations Online*, n.d., nationsonline.org. Accessed 8 Oct. 2024.

CHAPTER 2. GEOGRAPHY

1. Warren Moran and Conrad Alexander Blyth. "New Zealand." *Britannica*, 8 Oct. 2024, britannica.com. Accessed 16 Oct. 2024.
2. "New Zealand." *CIA World Factbook*, 1 Oct. 2024, cia.gov. Accessed 8 Oct. 2024.
3. Andrew Bain. "Beyond North and South: NZ's Incredible Forgotten 'Other Islands.'" *Sydney Morning Herald*, 4 Dec. 2023, smh.com.au. Accessed 8 Oct. 2024.
4. "North Island." *Britannica*, 9 Sept. 2024, britannica.com. Accessed 8 Oct. 2024.
5. "South Island." *Britannica*, 24 Sept. 2024, britannica.com. Accessed 8 Oct. 2024.
6. "New Zealand Climate and Weather." *Tourism New Zealand*, n.d., newzealand.com. Accessed 8 Oct. 2024.
7. "Weather and Climate in New Zealand." *Natural Habitat Adventures*, n.d., nathab.com. Accessed 8 Oct. 2024.
8. "*Chionochloa rubra subsp. cuprea*." *New Zealand Plant Conservation Network*, n.d., nzpcn.org.nz. Accessed 19 Nov. 2024.
9. Jacqui Gibson. "The Māori Tribe Protecting New Zealand's Sacred Rainforest." *BBC*, 9 June 2020, bbc.com. Accessed 8 Oct. 2024.
10. Lindsay Chatterton. "New Zealand." *Freshwater Ecoregions of the World*, n.d., feow.org. Accessed 8 Oct. 2024.
11. "New Zealand." *World Regional Geography*, 2016, open.lib.umn.edu. Accessed 8 Oct. 2024.
12. "Beech Forest." *Department of Conservation*, n.d., doc.govt.nz. Accessed 8 Oct. 2024.
13. "Glaciers in New Zealand." *Te Ara*, n.d., teara.govt.nz. Accessed 8 Oct. 2024.
14. "New Zealand," *CIA World Factbook*.
15. "New Zealand's Volcanoes." *Institute of Geological and Nuclear Sciences*, n.d., gns.cri.nz. Accessed 8 Oct. 2024.
16. "New Zealand's Volcanoes."
17. "New Zealand's Volcanoes."
18. "The Ring of Fire." *National Geographic*, n.d., nationalgeographic.com. Accessed 8 Oct. 2024.
19. "New Zealand's Volcanoes."
20. "New Zealand's Volcanoes."

CHAPTER 3. PLANTS AND ANIMALS

1. "New Zealand—Country Profile." *Convention on Biological Diversity*, n.d., cbd.int. Accessed 8 Oct. 2024.
2. "New Zealand—Country Profile."
3. "Tuatara." *San Diego Zoo Wildlife Alliance*, n.d., animals.sandiegozoo.org. Accessed 8 Oct. 2024.
4. "Tuatara." *Department of Conservation*, n.d., doc.govt.nz. Accessed 8 Oct. 2024.
5. "Long-Tailed Bat." *Department of Conservation*, n.d., doc.govt.nz. Accessed 8 Oct. 2024.
6. "Moa." *Britannica*, 17 Sept. 2024, britannica.com. Accessed 8 Oct. 2024.
7. "Kiwi." *San Diego Zoo Wildlife Alliance*, n.d., animals.sandiegozoo.org. Accessed 8 Oct. 2024.
8. "Takahē." *Department of Conservation*, n.d., doc.govt.nz. Accessed 8 Oct. 2024.
9. "Kākāpō." *Department of Conservation*, n.d., doc.govt.nz. Accessed 8 Oct. 2024.

10. "Morepork/Ruru." *Department of Conservation*, n.d., doc.govt.nz. Accessed 8 Oct. 2024.
11. "The Uniqueness of New Zealand's Plants." *Science Learning Hub*, 3 July 2018, sciencelearn.org.nz. Accessed 8 Oct. 2024.
12. "New Zealand's Marine Biodiversity." *Department of Conservation*, n.d., doc.govt.nz. Accessed 8 Oct. 2024.
13. "New Zealand's Marine Biodiversity."
14. "Hector's Dolphin." *National Oceanic and Atmospheric Administration Fisheries*, 8 Sept. 2022, fisheries.noaa.gov. Accessed 8 Oct. 2024.
15. "New Zealand's Marine Biodiversity."
16. "New Zealand's Marine Biodiversity."

CHAPTER 4. HISTORY

1. Magdalena M. E. Bunbury, Fiona Petchey, and Simon H. Bickler. "A New Chronology for the Māori Settlement of Aotearoa (NZ)." *Proceedings of the National Academy of Sciences of the United States of America*, 7 Nov. 2022, pnas.org. Accessed 8 Oct. 2024.
2. "The Arrival of Māori." *Tourism New Zealand*, n.d., newzealand.com. Accessed 8 Oct. 2024.
3. Danny Keenan. "New Zealand Wars." *Te Ara*, 29 Nov. 2022, teara.govt.nz. Accessed 8 Oct. 2024.
4. Keenan, "New Zealand Wars."
5. "The Treaty in Practice." *New Zealand History*, 5 Oct. 2021, nzhistory.govt.nz. Accessed 8 Oct. 2024.
6. "7.0 Quake Near Christchurch, New Zealand." *Earth Observatory*, n.d., earthobservatory.nasa.gov. Accessed 8 Oct. 2024.
7. Paul Dyer. "Policy and Institutional Responses to COVID-19: New Zealand." *Brookings Institution*, 24 Jan. 2021, brookings.edu. Accessed 8 Oct. 2024.
8. "Mortality Analyses." *Johns Hopkins University and Medicine*, 16 Mar. 2023, coronavirus.jhu.edu. Accessed 16 Dec. 2024.

CHAPTER 5. PEOPLE AND CULTURE

1. "New Zealand Population." *Worldometer*, n.d., worldometers.info. Accessed 8 Oct. 2024.
2. "New Zealand." *CIA World Factbook*, 1 Oct. 2024, cia.gov. Accessed 8 Oct. 2024.
3. "2023 Census Population Counts (By Ethnic Group, Age, and Māori Descent) and Dwelling Counts." *Stats NZ*, 29 May 2024, stats.govt.nz. Accessed 8 Oct. 2024.
4. "New Zealand Population."
5. "New Zealand."
6. "New Zealand."
7. "New Zealand."
8. "New Zealand."
9. "The Christchurch Mosque Attacks: How Parliament Responded." *New Zealand Parliament*, 15 Mar. 2024, parliament.nz. Accessed 8 Oct. 2024.
10. "Anzac Day." *New Zealand History*, 16 Apr. 2020, nzhistory.govt.nz. Accessed 8 Oct. 2024.
11. "The Artists." *Höglund Art Glass*, n.d., hoglundartglass.com. Accessed 8 Oct. 2024.
12. "Weaving Women." *Tourism New Zealand*, n.d., newzealand.com. Accessed 8 Oct. 2024.

SOURCE **NOTES** CONTINUED

CHAPTER 6. POLITICS

1. "Members of Parliament." *New Zealand Parliament*, n.d., parliament.nz. Accessed 8 Oct. 2024.
2. Chad de Guzman. "New Zealand's Youngest MP-Elect in 170 Years Is Māori and Proud—but Also Concerned." *Time*, 9 Nov. 2023, time.com. Accessed 8 Oct. 2024.
3. "New Zealand." *CIA World Factbook*, 1 Oct. 2024, cia.gov. Accessed 8 Oct. 2024.
4. "Queen Elizabeth II—Her Coronation and First Visit to New Zealand in 1953." *Museum of New Zealand*, n.d., tepapa.govt.nz. Accessed 8 Oct. 2024.
5. "Register of Political Parties." *Electoral Commission*, n.d., elections.nz. Accessed 8 Oct. 2024.

CHAPTER 7. ECONOMICS

1. "New Zealand." *CIA World Factbook*, 1 Oct. 2024, cia.gov. Accessed 8 Oct. 2024.
2. "Energy in New Zealand." *Ministry of Business, Innovation, and Employment*, Aug. 2022, mbie.govt.nz. Accessed 16 Dec. 2024.
3. "The History of Ironsand." *New Zealand Steel*, n.d., nzsteel.co.nz. Accessed 8 Oct. 2024.
4. "New Zealand Gold Production." *CEIC*, n.d., ceicdata.com. Accessed 8 Oct. 2024.
5. "Māori Farm Size Much Larger than Average Size." *Stats NZ*, 29 Aug. 2023, stats.govt.nz. Accessed 8 Oct. 2024.
6. L. Granwal. "Dairy Industry in New Zealand." *Statista*, 14 Feb. 2024, statista.com. Accessed 8 Oct. 2024.
7. L. Granwal. "Number of Sheep Livestock in New Zealand from 2011 to 2023." *Statista*, 2 Feb. 2024, statista.com. Accessed 8 Oct. 2024.
8. Harrison Wade. "Kiwis Own the Most Cars per Capita in the World, New Data Shows." *New Zealand Autocar Magazine*, 23 Feb. 2024, autocar.co.nz. Accessed 8 Oct. 2024.
9. "Length of Roads in New Zealand." *Figure.NZ*, 27 Sept. 2024, figure.nz. Accessed 8 Oct. 2024.
10. "Airlines Serving New Zealand." *Ministry of Transport*, n.d., transport.govt.nz. Accessed 8. Oct. 2024.
11. "Convert United States Dollar to New Zealand Dollar." *Forbes*, n.d., forbes.com. Accessed 8 Oct. 2024.
12. "Energy in New Zealand." *Ministry of Business, Innovation, and Employment*, Aug. 2023, mbie.govt.nz. Accessed 8 Oct. 2024.
13. "Tracking Planting for the One Billion Trees Programme." *Ministry for Primary Industries*, 30 Sept. 2024, mpi.govt.nz. Accessed 19 Nov. 2024.

CHAPTER 8. NEW ZEALAND TODAY

1. "NZR Encouraging Small Steps in New Mental Wellbeing Campaign." *New Zealand Rugby*, 8 Sept. 2021, nzrugby.co.nz. Accessed 8 Oct. 2024.
2. "Female Rugby Player Numbers Rise but Males in Decline." *Radio New Zealand*, 14 Nov. 2023, rnz.co.nz. Accessed 8 Oct. 2024.
3. "About the Team." *Black Ferns*, n.d., allblacks.com. Accessed 8 Oct. 2024.
4. "Early Childhood Education." *Ministry of Education*, 19 Aug. 2024, education.govt.nz. Accessed 16 Dec. 2024.
5. "3-B-4 Home-Based ECE Services." *Ministry of Education*, 1 Jan. 2025, education.govt.nz. Accessed 8 Jan. 2025.
6. Vitas Carosella. "Rugby in New Zealand: A Door to Women's Participation." *Sport and Dev*, 14 Mar. 2023, sportanddev.org. Accessed 8 Oct. 2024.
7. "About NCEA." *Ministry of Education*, n.d., ncea.education.govt.nz. Accessed 19 Nov. 2024.
8. "The School System." *Live and Work New Zealand*, n.d., live-work.immigration.govt.nz. Accessed 8 Oct. 2024.
9. "Tuition Fees and Cost of Living." *Think New*, n.d., studywithnewzealand.govt.nz. Accessed 19 Nov. 2024.
10. "Study and Train at Universities." *Tertiary Education Commission*, 11 July 2024, careers.govt.nz. Accessed 19 Nov. 2024.
11. Einar H. Dyvik. "Proportion of Children Living in Poverty in OECD Countries in 2022." *Statista*, 4 July 2024, statista.com. Accessed 8 Oct. 2024.
12. "Child Poverty." *Organisation for Economic Co-operation and Development Family Database*, n.d., oecd.org. Accessed 8 Oct. 2024.
13. Gurjit Kaur, Kathryn Fox, and Ailsa Chang. "A Breakdown of the Issues at the Center of Maori Protests in New Zealand." *National Public Radio*, 8 Dec. 2023, npr.org. Accessed 8 Oct. 2024.
14. "Tourism Impact." *Tourism New Zealand Corporate Website*, n.d., tourismnewzealand.com. Accessed 8 Oct. 2024.
15. "National Parks." *Tourism New Zealand*, n.d., newzealand.com. Accessed 16 Dec. 2024.
16. "National Parks."
17. "New Zealand to Nearly Triple Tourist Tax for International Visitors." *Guardian*, 3 Sept. 2024, theguardian.com. Accessed 8 Oct. 2024.
18. "The Problem with 'Overtourism'—and How to Address It." *Radio New Zealand*, 5 June 2024, rnz.co.nz. Accessed 8 Oct. 2024.

INDEX

ABOUT THE **AUTHOR**

SUE BRADFORD EDWARDS

Sue Bradford Edwards is a nonfiction author who writes from her home office in Missouri. Her favorite topics include cultures, history, ancient peoples, and wildlife. She is the author of 30 other titles from Abdo Publishing, including *Russia*, *Australia*, *Ancient Maya*, and *Hidden Human Computers*. She corresponds with classmates and fellow writers across the United States and all over the world, including a friend in New Zealand, but her favorite place of all is in the alpine desert of West Texas.